Where Waterfalls and Wild Things Are

Exploring Waterfalls, Swimming Holes and Wild, Scenic Places in the Southeastern Olympics

Mark Woytowich

Where Waterfalls and Wild Things Are

All Rights Reserved © 2019 by Mark Woytowich

Published by Mark Woytowich

For Volney Rogers

"When our eyes follow the flow of a waterfall,
we are treated to something both moving and solid,
fleeting yet eternal, and composed of millions of
droplets that unite in a single form. When a thing
can be two ways at once, it is said to be magic . . .
and if not magic, then at least a key into the doorway
of illusion, truth, and art, and the many reasons for
why a thing is beautiful to us, or makes us cry."

Preface

A note to lovers of wild things, wherever they are

Exploring is an obsession. This book is the culmination of a 25-year obsession with the waterfalls, swimming holes, hidden canyons and other priceless gems of the southern Olympic Mountain Range.

It is a book written for my fellow fanatics out there, the men and women who will scramble over boulders, hike off trail, and generally risk the cuts, bruises and scrapes you sometimes acquire when you bushwhack your way to "the waterfall *behind* the waterfall," and other beautiful places that can only be found by exploring further than the commonly known trail.

If you are a true fanatic (or more likely a normal person who carries a fanatic around inside himself), then you will not focus on the "risk" side of the equation, but instead, on the vast, unspeakable rewards of finding paradise-like places merely by going around the next bend.

It really happens like that. A small, peaceful creek will lead you to a staggering, sumptuous waterfall. A faded goat trail will suddenly take you to a swimming hole so deep, calm and pristine that you will swear angels and kings and gods must gather there to bathe and discuss philosophy.

This has been my reality for many seasons. This book is for explorers and nature lovers, the kind of people who appreciate and understand why you will hike up a rocky canyon because up there, somewhere, is a waterfall, a place, a view so special that, while maybe it can be described, is only ever truly known by sitting there and seeing it, and taking it in on that soul level whereby a canyon like the Grand Canyon or a waterfall like Yosemite literally stuns us with their beauty.

By writing this book, I leave you with the means to take on these quests, one waterfall, one swimming hole, one wild thing at a time.

OMMISSIONS

In Chapter 18 on Watson Falls, I did not provide a description of the main trail you pick up from the crosswalk on the Hamma Hamma Road. Frankly, I was not concerned with mentioning much about the Living Legacy Trail in this book.

In fact, this book will be skipping over many trails throughout the National Park and Forest because, for one thing, I do not want to write about a place that is already well documented elsewhere.

Secondly, as the title suggests, the emphasis of this book is on "where the wild things are."

I prefer the path not taken. Yes, a monstrous cliché but, nevertheless, I feel the value of what I am trying to share with you is that this material covers new or relatively unexplored places of interest.

So much is already known and available about the Living Legacy Trail. The same can be said about Staircase Loop Trail, Wagonwheel Lake Trail, Dry Creek Trail, Mt. Rose Trail, and a host of others. Because this book doesn't allow the time and space to cover every trail around, I need to omit or skim quickly over those trails and destinations you can research elsewhere.

Remember, this book is about waterfalls. Especially the lesser known and out-of-the-way waterfalls and places of beauty.

MAPLE FIRE OMISSIONS

Finally, please read carefully the beginning of Chapter 25, which explains briefly the effects of the 2018 Maple Fire, and how limited access to the Jefferson Creek Watershed will make it impossible to describe, up-to-date, the conditions of all eight scenic destinations located there.

Table of Contents

Getting Started

1a. Introduction 8
1b. Be Prepared 10

Main Map. 13
"Traveler's Table" Map Key 14

Dosewallips River and Duckabush River Watersheds

2. Rocky Brook Falls &
    Swimming Hole 18
3. Dosewallips scenic views. 20
4. Murhut Falls 22

5. Duckabush Swimming Hole. . .24
6. Duckabush Delta 25
7. Ranger Hole Trail & Canyon . . .26

Hamma Hamma River Watershed

8. Upper Hamma Hamma Falls . 30
9. Lower Hamma Hamma Falls
    & Swimming Hole. 32
10. Beaver Pond Trail 34
11. Hamma Hamma Bottoms. . .35
12. Goat Trail above Lena Creek . 36
13. Lena Creek Campground
    & River Access 37
14. Lena Lake 38
15. Cabin Creek Falls 40

16. The art of Canyoneering 42
17. Zip Line Canyon. 44
18. Watson Creek Falls 46
19. Four Mile Falls. 48
20. Waketickeh Creek 49
21. Upper Jorstad Falls. 52
22. Washington Pass (FR #2441) 54
23. Craig's Beach, Lilliwaup 56
24. Lilliwaup Falls. 58

Jefferson Creek Watershed

25a. The 2018 Maple Fire. 64
25b. Elk Lake Trail. 65
26. The Balds, Alternate
    Elk Lake Trail 66
27. Upper Elk Lake 69
28. Upper Washington
    Creek Swimming Hole. 71

29. Washington Creek Swimming
    Hole & Canyon 74
30. Lower Jefferson Falls
    and campsites 76
31. Boulder Field - Jefferson Lake . 78
32. Upper Jefferson Falls 82
33. Little Yosemite 86

North Fork Skokomish River Watershed

34. Mt. Ellinor 90
35. Big Creek Falls - Jefferson Pass
      to Mt. Washington 92
36. Big Creek Confluence & Trail . . 96
37. Dow Mountain 98
38. Cushman Falls -
      Mt. Rose Trailhead 100
39. Lake Cushman Swim Spots . . 102
40. Shady Lane Trail to
      Staircase Loop 104
41. Copper Creek Mines & Trail . . 107
42. Alley Falls - Snow Lake Falls . 109

South Fork Skokomish River Watershed

43. Vincent Creek Falls
      & High Steel Bridge. 114
44. Vance Creek Bridge 116
45. Rock Creek Falls & Canyon . . 119
46. Oxbow Campground &
      River Rafting 121
47. Lower South Fork Skokomish
      Trail & Swimmng Hole 124
48. Spider Lake & Falls 128

Wynoochee River Watershed

49. Truman Glick Park 132
50. John Tornow Grave &
      Shootout Site. 134
51. "Ring of Fire" Locomotive
      Wreck Site. 138
52. Wynoochee River, Lake
      & Dam 141
53. Maidenhair Falls. 143
54. Wynoochee Falls 145
55. Spoon Creek Falls 147

Other Wild Places of Interest

56. Fudge Point Beach. 150
57. Goldsborough Creek
      Otterfalls 152

In closing

58. Waterfall Witness Protection Program 155

1a/ Introduction

The interior of the Olympic Mountain Range was one of the last regions to be explored by white men in the continental United States. A rugged mass of snowy peaks isolated from any other mountain chain, they were not crossed, east to west, until 1890, when Lieutenant Joseph O'Neill led his expedition up the North Fork Skokomish River, eventually reaching the Pacific Coast after a long and laborious journey.

Seen from space, the Olympics form a round circle of mountain ridges, with Mt. Olympus, roughly in the middle, topping out at 7,980 feet. Though the Olympics stretch less than 70 miles across, more than a dozen major rivers run down from their uppermost slopes, fanning out in all directions like watery spokes from a glacier-hubbed wheel.

Most of these rivers run less than 30 miles in length; a few, like the Hamma Hamma and Duckabush, are much shorter than that. Now, add to this picture the fact that the Olympic Peninsula is one of the wettest zones in North America, and what that means, essentially, is that a whole lot of water travels a very short distance to reach sea level on all sides.

With such extreme elevation drop--8,000 feet to zero in just a few miles--you have the basic formula for waterfalls everywhere. And while the Olympics do not feature, by any means, the top-rated or highest waterfalls in the Pacific Northwest, they nevertheless host an abundance of prominent, classic beauties such as Sol Duc Falls, Marymere Falls, Rocky Brook Falls, Murhut Falls, and at least three dozen others worth exploring.

Fortunately for residents and visitors of Hood Canal and the southeastern Olympics, many of the best waterfalls--as well as swimming holes and scenic canyons--reside within the south-to-southeast quadrant of the Olympic Peninsula. Better yet, most require only a short hike or drive on a gravel mountain road to reach them.

This book was written to bring viewers and lovers of nature closer to the objects they desire. In particular, I want waterfall and swimming hole devotees to discover and appreciate the many breath-taking treasures awaiting them on America's publicly funded land.

Indeed, as public treasures, they are yours to enjoy. At the same time, you need to do your part in maintaining their beauty. In no way should you leave trash of any kind behind after a visit. Pick up after pets. Never build a fire except in an existing fire pit. Never take a motorized vehicle on a designated foot path. When car camping (also known as dispersed camping), please try to use existing sites and campfire rings. Never cut living trees for firewood.

Paying attention and "leaving no trace" are the way of life for responsible visitors of national forest and national park lands. They are not hard rules to follow. In fact, they are badges of honor for those who truly love America and her pristine public lands. Showing respect and kindness toward nature sets a strong example for those who may not yet know how to keep our forests clean.

How would you treat and leave your own back yard?

In bringing these treasures to you, I open ways to places of beauty for those who would normally have passed them by. While I cannot choose the characters and temperaments of the visitors I inspire, I trust the good will outnumber the careless, and thoughtful, responsible citizens will outnumber the fools.

Prove me right, okay?

Old weathered footbridge on Big Creek Trail

1b/ Prepare before departing

Spoon Creek Falls has four tiers, with its tallest section dropping straight down onto a ledge, and then spilling out from there one more time, white water gushing over a final sculpted layer.

On one of my most recent visits to the falls, a good friend of mine climbed the slippery ledge that forms the lowest stage of the falls, intending to join me at the back of the ledge where the main plunge-- about 80 feet--roars straight down into a bathtub-sized hole in the rock, where it churns with a fury, a veritable Mother Nature's whirlpool tub.

The ledge is only 12 feet high but would not make a good place for falling. If you lost your balance and slid off, the rocks and shallow water below would embrace you with a serious bruising at best, and quite likely result in a broken limb or worse, if you landed awkwardly.

Working his fingers along the rock and his toes on the narrow shelf below, my friend "spider crawled" sideways along the ledge, looking down for toe holds, up for hand moves, crossing steadily until he stood beside me.

"Whew," he said, "finally safe."

Then he held out his cell phone.

This was the craziest thing I ever saw. The falls were whipping up a rainstorm right there on the ledge--a vortex of windy weather--with the force of many firehoses blasting straight down, 80 feet, smacking and churning up the "bath tub," kicking up a mist that chilled my skin and drenched my eyes. We had to shout to hear each other.

In the midst of this storm, you want to snap a photo?

Okay, I get it. Cell phone is camera. Camera makes memories. This is really cool, about to jump into Mother Nature's whirlpool, a perfect moment for a selfie, right?

No, not exactly.

He might as well drop his phone in a bucket of water. No way could that little piece of electronic equipment stay dry and operational in the spray zone. Even worse, he set his phone, face up, on the rocks when he plunged into the falls.

And while he loved the sensation of jumping into the cold, swirling water, he did it at the cost of his smart phone.

Not so smart when you say bye-bye to a vital communication tool.

WHAT ARE THE VARIABLES?

Now, the point of this unfortunate but true tale is to alert you as to what to expect when you visit each and every one of the destinations recommended in this book.

While this book cannot anticipate or eliminate every possible variable you may encounter, I hope my descriptions, maps and key symbols help you understand what kind of adventures you are signing up for.

For instance, let's say you decide to visit Upper Jefferson Falls and are not a seasoned hiker or very experienced with getting around the Olympics. Without the "heads up" information in this guide, you might be in for a long series of surprises, starting with snow level, road conditions, difficulty of climb, and fear factor related to the trail's proximity to danger.

The point I'm trying to make is that I don't want you bringing your cell phone to a place that can cause it harm. Nor do I want you bringing your new car to a place where you shouldn't drive it, or your kids to a ledge where they may get hurt.

Start off well informed, and you'll be better prepared to have successful adventures.

ODOMETER IS KING

This guidebook is intended to do more than just list the names of waterfalls and show you pictures. In *Where Waterfalls and Wild Things Are*, you will be given a sense of why a certain place is special or beautiful, and exactly how and when you may approach it.

In nearly all cases, I will cite a point at which you are to set your car's odometer to zero. It is very important to do this. An accurate odometer reading will eliminate the guesswork in finding a trailhead, parking spot, or other landmark of importance.

PUSH YOURSELF

Lastly before we begin: you most definitely can enjoy this book as a pure armchair experience. In describing what are truly amazing places, I hope my words are strong and clear enough to capture your imagination. If you are gaining years or gaining weight, simply too senior, too out of shape, injured or otherwise unable to go on these hikes and adventures, then this book should still prove to be a fun and exciting read.

Also, if you've been to these places long ago, or have heard about them in local lore or from old timers spinning their yarns, you may enjoy reading about them so that you, too, can affirm their legacy.

In the same way that many people in Mason County still cherish the old logging days, stories of outlaw John Tornow, tales of the Mosquito Fleet and Antlers Hotel, many people are equally proud to know about the fabulous waterfalls and wild places around Hood Canal.

Please, if you can, try to get to as many of these spots as possible. Push yourself a little if you need to. You won't regret any day that you hiked long and hard to reach a gorgeous goal. Believe me, despite whatever stiffness or soreness you may feel the following morning, you will absolutely glow with satisfaction from achieving your destination. You might even develop a taste for a certain "good" stiffness you feel after a strenuous hike. It's your body's way of thanking you for taking it out on a date, a very physical date. Your body is telling you, hey, let's do this again, my friend.

Hundreds of times I've guided people to some pretty whacky and way out places, and asked them to swim in cold water or hike across a flowing creek. Never did I hear that they were sorry they came, or regretted trying something a little bit beyond their norm.

I hope you will invite change and challenge into your life. While your personal safety and the choices you must make will always be yours to decide alone, I want you to stay open to new ideas, places, and possible ways of doing things.

With *Where Waterfalls and Wild Things Are* as your guide, you will certainly have plenty of tempting places to explore. May you take on whatever you set out to do. May each accomplishment give you added courage to go beyond your limits. Most important of all, with every waterfall or swimming hole you visit, may your love and appreciation for our scenic treasures grow more strong.

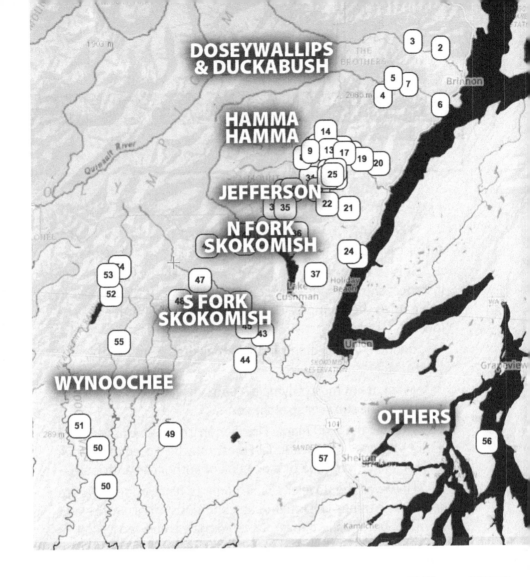

SECTIONS BY WATERSHEDS

Dosewallips & Duckabush   16
Hamma Hamma River 28
Jefferson Creek 62
North Fork Skokomish . . . 88
South Fork Skokomish . . 112
Wynoochee 130
Others. 149

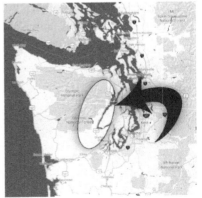

SEASONAL CONCERNS	ROAD CONDITIONS	TRAIL DIFFICULTY	SAFETY CONCERNS	TRAILHEAD PASS?

TRAVELER'S TABLE

The above "Traveler's Table" is an aid to help you quickly surmise whether a particular trip is going to be your "cup of tea."

It is by no means an accurate gauge of all the variables. For instance, snowy roads may stay snow-covered much longer in one part of the Olympics, despite the fact their altitude may be lower.

Sudden, unexpected rains can make roads impassable any time of year.

Many, if not most, Olympic Mountain waterfalls diminish in volume as the summer stretches on.

And, as the 2018 Maple Fire demonstrates to this very day, entire sections of the National Forest may be closed to visitors, and for a length of time that no book or author can anticipate.

However, the Traveler's Table ought to help you stay alert to some basic things like rough road conditions, cliffs, swift water or other potentially dangerous conditions--and most vital of all--what kind of trailhead pass may be required to spare you a nasty little ticket on your windshield.

For simplicity, I've tried to avoid acronyms and abbreviations. Following is your key to all the information that might show up in each chapter's Traveler's Table.

Snowy road on way to "Little Yosemite" Valley, just past Upper Jefferson Falls

TRAVELER'S TABLE: Categories Defined

SEASONAL CONCERNS

ALL SEASON = Road normally open and free of snow

SNOW LEVEL = Road(s) may be blocked or difficult due to seasonal snow

HIGH WATER = Canyon exploring may be more difficult if river or stream level is too high

FALLS DIMINISH = Waterfall magnificence lessens with lower seasonal flows

FALLS RUN DRY = Waterfall may be gone by summer

ROAD CONDITIONS

DECENT ROADS = Destination is approachable by any kind of car

POTHOLES = Nasty for any kind of vehicle

4WD = Recommend four-wheel drive due to loose rocks, potential snow, general "rutty" nature of road

ROUGH ROAD = Challenging driving, even for 4WD

TRAIL DIFFICULTY

EASY = Anyone in decent health ought to be able to reach the destination

EASY-MODERATE = Possibly challenging if you are not in shape

MODERATE = Expect a decent workout, some altitude or incline, but attainable for those in shape

DIFFICULT = Strong, challenging climb

CANYON = Designates a canyoneering experience of walking through moving water

SAFETY CONCERNS

SAFE = Either no danger or danger is very apparent and avoidable

PICNIC SAFE = Better than safe, this is a family-friendly destination with a picnic suitable place

KID CAUTION = Journey or destination requires awareness of surroundings, and guidance of small feet

WATER CROSSING = Typically an easy, shallow-water canyoneering experience (Mild Kid Caution)

SWIFT WATER = Challenging canyon with boulder obstacles (Kid Caution)

CLIFFS = Dangerous trail sections with sheer drop-off (Strong Kid Caution)

TRAILHEAD PASS?

NONE = No pass required

FOREST PASS = NW Forest Pass (Day: $5.00 or Annual: $30.00) Purchase at Olympic National Forest ranger stations or visitor centers.

DISCOVER = Washington State Parks Discover Pass (Day: $10.00; Annual for $35.00 if purchased at visitor centers, find day passes at some trailheads or parking lots).

From Top: Unnamed seasonal waterfall on Dosewallips Trail in Olympic National Park, riverside campsite at Elkhorn Campground, mists and clouds over Duckabush River bridge.

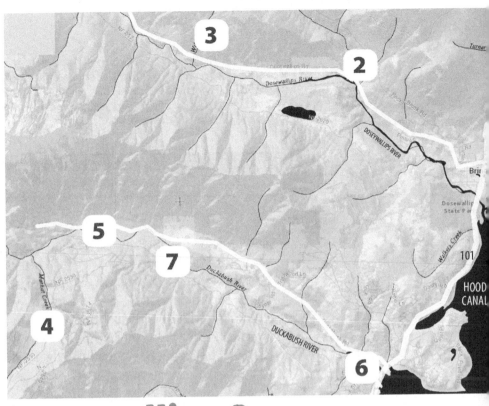

Dosewallips & Duckabush Watersheds

2 Rocky Brook Falls 18
3 Dosewallips scenic views . . . 20
4 Murhut Falls 22
5 Duckabush swimming hole. . 24
6 Duckabush Delta 25
7 Ranger Hole Canyon 26

2/Rocky Brook Falls

DIRECTIONS

From US Highway 101 in Brinnon, just north of the community center, turn into the entrance to Dosewallips Recreation Area. SET ODOMETER. In exactly 3 miles you'll cross a small bridge. Park just beyond it, and pick up the path beside the small power station.

SEASONAL CONCERNS	ROAD CONDITIONS	TRAIL DIFFICULTY	SAFETY CONCERNS	TRAILHEAD PASS?
ALL SEASON	DECENT ROAD	EASY	SAFE	NONE

*Definitions of Terms: Pages 14-15

Rocky Brook Falls is estimated to be from 130 to 170 feet high. Knowing the exact height is hardly the matter, as Rocky Brook is breathtakingly tall and beautiful with tumbling white braids sliding down her near-vertical rock face. In summer her watery strings bounce off staggered ledges while fanning to a wide apron, where she finally spills into an idyllic swimming hole.

With a simple scramble over a few ledges, you can walk right up and put your hands to her face, leaning, if you choose, into the base of the falls and cupping handfuls of water splashing down. From here, looking up, you cannot see the top of her spill, much as visitors to the Empire State Building cannot see its top from the sidewalk directly below.

Rocky Brook has two different personalities, however. Winter rains have her roaring at full gale, with so much water

LEFT: In summer the pool below Rocky Brook Falls gets warm enough for swimming, with large crowds to be expected on weekends.

crashing along her base that it kicks up a wind--a very wet wind--chilling your face and hands, and misting over the lenses of cameras and cell phones with her blowing spray. You dare not walk up and touch her when she pours this way.

In summer Rocky Brook flows much lower. Then she becomes a top swimming attraction, with afternoon sun crossing her face and helping to heat the water of her 8-foot-deep swimming hole. Ledges provide diving platforms of up to 15 feet, and water flows through well worn channels, providing "otter slides" for smaller bodies to plummet downwards. Popularity has its price, unfortunately; on hot summer weekends, expect large crowds.

THE DRIVE, THE TRAIL

Rocky Brook Falls lies north of Mason County, only 3 miles from US Highway 101 in Brinnon. (Ten minutes further north, another waterfall, Falls View Falls, waits at the end of an easy, short hike in the seasonally closed Falls View Campground. Tall and pretty, she runs dry in summer, however.)

The trail to Rocky Brook is a quarter-mile long and easy. You'll pass a small, private hydropower station on your left, with the brook on your right. You come up to the falls quite quickly and might need to scramble over several boulders, moving away from the falls, to get a good photo with the entire falls in frame.

Caution: In winter all the rocks are wet from spray, and the chance of twisting an ankle or slipping and falling is very real. Go slow.

Near the parking area, a gated dirt road leads upward and upstream from the top of the falls. This is private property, however, and is not recommended as a touring trail.

In summary: Rocky Brook is one of the top five waterfalls on the Olympic Peninsula. From July onwards, the temperature of her swimming hole grows surprisingly warm (in comparison to most Northwest falls and streams). She should rank highly as a "bucket list visit" for collectors of wild, authentic adventures, and also be seriously considered for an envigorating summertime swim.

3/Dosewallips Scenic Views

DIRECTIONS

Same as for previous chapter. Continue past Rocky Brook Falls, going another 3.3 miles to first stop. It is 8.6 miles, total, to end of road.

SEASONAL CONCERNS	ROAD CONDITIONS	TRAIL DIFFICULTY	SAFETY CONCERNS	TRAILHEAD PASS?
ALL SEASON	DECENT ROAD	EASY	CLIFFS	NONE

Definitions of Terms: Pages 14-15

This short trip is recommended for visitors who have already seen Rocky Brook Falls but are still curious about what lies further up the road.

With your odometer at 3 miles (right?) continue up the valley, keeping an eye out for elk that forage here in winter. Right away you start getting views of the Dosewallips River on your left. However, your first and main stop will be at the pullout marked by large boulders at 6.3 miles. Look to your left for a pair of bare spots beside the road with a mighty big rock sticking up between them.

You'll undoubtedly hear the roar of the river the moment you step from your car. Climb straight up that big rock and approach the edge, carefully.

Twenty feet below you is a very deep "swimming" hole. That word lies in quotation marks because this is hardly the place for a peaceful swim. And while I don't doubt that someone, somewhere, has jumped off this rock and come back out of that water safely, I would rate both that person and their experience as highly unusual.

No, this spot is more for viewing, not swimming. The combination of deep water and strong current guarantee that this spot will put an "instant snap" into the nerves of anyone who enters the water suddenly, because cold, moving water has a greater chill factor than water that is still. There is a very real chance of going into shock.

Take a moment and look around this awesome little canyon. Observe the white froth where the rapids turn. Look at the effects of water eroding rock over time: worn, round niches in the boulders, shallow caves, craggy, half-hidden beaches where smaller rocks come to rest.

Short paths on the right lead to a lower, safer ledge. From here you can sit and truly take in the view. And yes, if you're like me, you can look up and down at the sheer cliffs on each side, imagining what it would be like to plunge into the mighty Dosewallips River.

NEW WASHOUT

Continue up the road until it becomes unpaved at 6.8 miles. Some excellent views are just ahead, but you may want to weigh the cost/benefit of continuing, as the road gets a little rough. Not quite 4WD territory, but still a consideration.

In less than two miles the road will dead-end at a washout just before the Tunnel Creek Trail. This remains a popular parking spot for backpackers going into or coming out of Olympic National Park.

I'm encouraging you to check out the road to its end, as many pullouts on the left serve both as scenic views, plus overnight camping sites especially suited for campers and small trailers. Dispersed camping this way in the national forest is free, by the way.

A quick roadside stop gets you an admirable view of the Dosewallips River coursing through a small canyon three miles up the road beyond Rocky Brook Falls.

4/Murhut Falls

DIRECTIONS

Take Highway 101 north toward Brinnon. After crossing the Duckabush River Bridge, make a left onto Duckabush Road. SET ODOMETER. At six miles you will pass the Duckabush Trailhead on your right, then cross the Duckabush River again. Just after this second bridge the road forks. Take the right fork, following the sign 1.2 miles uphill to the marked trailhead and parking spot for Murhut Falls.

SEASONAL CONCERNS	ROAD CONDITIONS	TRAIL DIFFICULTY	SAFETY CONCERNS	TRAILHEAD PASS?
SNOW LEVEL	DECENT/ 4WD	EASY-MODERATE	MILD KID CAUTION	NONE

*Definitions of Terms: Pages 14-15

Magical Murhut Falls is one of the Big Six Waterfalls located the eastern half of the Olympic Mountains--six waterfalls that stand proudly as "Must See's" for anyone interested in splendor and beauty.

Moving counter-clockwise from north to south, they are: Rocky Brook Falls; Murhut Falls; Hamma Hamma Falls; Lilliwaup Falls; Vincent Creek Falls and Spoon Creek Falls.

Compared to Rocky Brook, Murhut Falls takes a little more work to see and enjoy, but its size, beauty and serene location make it, in my opinion, the most majestic of all the Big Six Falls.

TALE OF THE TRAIL

It's a one-mile hike from the trailhead to Murhut, with the first two-thirds a gradual, steady climb. The incline is not difficult for the young or fit, but might be a slight challenge if you're not in shape.

If you're a trail runner, the trail to Murhut is wonderful, wide, and well-maintained--perfect for sprinting to the falls and then rewarding yourself with a cool splash in Murhut's lower pool. Or, walk slowly and in 15 minutes simply enjoy the falls from the viewing bench at the end of the trail; often the best photos are taken here.

You'll hear Murhut before you see her. The trail rounds the ridge at it's highest point, then winds downhill until you see her across a mossy, boulder strewn gorge. From where she breaks atop a forested hill, she thunders 90 feet over a rock face, churning into a shallow, upper pool with a fairly large cave lurking behind her curtain of falling water.

From here, Murhut turns to plunge down another 35 feet over a mossy shelf, dropping into a boulder bejeweled creek with many pools and cataracts. Fallen, giant firs and cedars make footbridges and sitting benches across the gorge.

You can climb a knotted, octopus-like root wad to ascend the far hillside, which will take you to the upper falls. Likewise, you can "boulder" your way (that is, scramble over rocks and boulders) to visit three smaller waterfalls and Shangri-La swimming holes just downstream. If you are good in bare feet or with wet sandals or tennis shoes, I highly recommend going downstream, as it is a most pleasant puzzle to work you way to and from the lower falls.

GORGE DESCENT

All the foot traffic going in and out of the gorge has created some loose soil and "chancy" looking ways to descend. Go to the furthest point on the trail, past the bench on your left, and drop down there, holding onto the roots and descending backwards, NOT facing the falls. Piece of cake.

Murhut is a very family-friendly destination, supporting swimmers, photographers and long picnic lunches. The site draws visitors from all over the world. You can feel a primitive, deep green beauty here, the rainforest's wet and naked soul.

5/Duckabush Swimming Hole

DIRECTIONS

Take Highway 101 north toward Brinnon. After crossing the Duckabush River Bridge, make a left onto Duckabush Road. SET ODOMETER. At six miles you will pass the Duckabush Trailhead on your right, then cross the upper Duckabush River Bridge.

SEASONAL CONCERNS	ROAD CONDITIONS	TRAIL DIFFICULTY	SAFETY CONCERNS	TRAILHEAD PASS?
ALL SEASON	DECENT/ POTHOLES	EASY	DEEP WATER	NONE

Definitions of Terms: Pages 14-15

Save this spot for the hottest of days. Six miles up the Duckabush Road, you cross the river on a concrete bridge. You need to park just before or after the bridge and come to the railing to look downstream. If it's hot enough, you might catch a glimpse of bathers enjoying what I call the Duckabush Swimming Hole.

On the upstream side of the bridge, a short trail leads you to a ledge below the bridge, where you should find a rope swing waiting for you.

It's plenty deep and clear here; far deep enough to jump safely from the bridge, a challenging 20-plus foot drop. In summer the water is cold but not prohibitively frigid.

To reach the swimming hole, backtrack along the river side of the road prior to the bridge, until you see a trail leading down to the water. This is a beautiful family-friendly spot that allows for deep swimming or shallow sunning, and, if you're not a local, it deserves an extra measure of respect: be patient, be kind, be picking up after yourself.

6/Duckabush Delta

DIRECTIONS
The Duckabush River Bridge is on Highway 101 a few miles south of Brinnon. The trail is on the north side of the bridge.

SEASONAL CONCERNS	ROAD CONDITIONS	TRAIL DIFFICULTY	SAFETY CONCERNS	TRAILHEAD PASS?
ALL SEASON	DECENT ROAD	EASY	WATER CROSSINGS	NONE

Definitions of Terms: Pages 14-15

Serious photographers, I promise you some incredible, dramatic shots but you'll need to time things right.

At low tide in late spring--Mid-April through May--the Duckabush Delta is teeming with life of every variety, ducks, herons, eagles and some of the biggest bumblebees I've ever seen hopping from flower to flower. Hummingbirds flash past and red winged blackbirds rattle their territorial cries.

Tall grasses and reeds make this a savannah-like experience.

Of course early light is best but just about anytime is good if you can pick up the Wildlife Preserve trail on the north side of the Highway 101 Duckabush Bridge, and follow that muddy, jungle-like track to where the river meets the Canal.

Remember, you're crossing tidelands so be ready for your share of muck. For guidance, you can preview the trail on Google Maps.

PANORAMIC PLEASURES

Now, the further you work your way down the delta, the wider the Olympic Mountain panorama will be to the west, including snow on the peaks, which, in photography terms, is literally icing on the cake.

Huge driftwood trees and logs rest at the mouth of the river. Line these up to frame your photos of the twin rainbow arches of the Duckabush Bridge.

For best results, you may need to get into the water, so prepare by wearing (or bringing) rubber sandals or tennis shoes that can get wet.

Low tide with good light, far out into the Canal--you'll be experiencing the kayaker's view, which is one of tidal connection and vast, windswept distances. Trust me, an hour out here and you'll grow wider, too, with perhaps your own panoramic glow.

7/Ranger Hole Canyon

DIRECTIONS

It is 22 miles from Hoodsport north to the Duckabush Road. Warning: a NW Forest Pass is a MUST for the trailhead.

SEASONAL CONCERNS	ROAD CONDITIONS	TRAIL DIFFICULTY	SAFETY CONCERNS	TRAILHEAD PASS?
HIGH WATER	DECENT ROAD	EASY-MODERATE	SWIFT WATER CLIFFS	FOREST PASS

*Definitions of Terms: Pages 14-15

If you're looking for a gorgeous yet easy hike, your choice of two swimming holes, flat rocks for a sunny picnic, and a waterfall with 20-foot diving cliffs beside it, read on.

Drive 3.6 miles up the Duckabush Road and park at the water pump beside the historic 1907 Interrorem Cabin, a cozy, for-rent hideaway.

The one-mile trek to Ranger Hole is an easy walk through a fairy tale forest. The trail shares the first hundred feet or so with the Interrorem Interpretive Nature Loop Trail before that trail branches to the left.

Stay right. Immediately, the forest grows dense, dark and immensely quiet. Large second growth firs mix with big leaf maples, their arms sleeved with moss. Sunlight barely speckles through the screen of trees above.

Thick ferns clump beside the trail. Old growth stumps still jut out from where the saw blade found them a hundred years ago, many sprouting new trees from their tops.

The trail ascends a series of steps, then gradually descends in a gentle, straight walkway through the heart of classic Northwest rainforest. Moss beds stretch as far as you can see, rolling out like thick green mats among vine maple, huckleberry, old logs and solitary, mossy stones.

You can cup the silence in your hands. Get ready to be surprised by bright green tree frogs and rather large toads.

The last section of trail runs steep with loose soil and might be challenging for hikers expecting traction. Descend sideways. Soon you will arrive at the rocky bluff overlooking legendary Ranger Hole.

Here a small waterfall spills into a deep swimming hole topped by 20-foot cliffs safe for jumping. It makes a great picnic spot and cool dip for hot weather, but is dangerous, in my opinion, for small children.

WHAT LIES UPSTREAM

From the high point above the falls at Ranger Hole, look upstream. Not far beyond the last visible batch of rapids, the river calms and forms a placid mini-fjord, a magnificent jade-colored channel flowing between smooth rocky bluffs.

Up there is a swimming hole and meditation spot like no other. During low late summer flows, the river averages about 6 feet deep––the same height as your jump from the bluffs. The water is ghostly green yet clear.

Bring an inflatable raft. You'll spend the entire day on it, hand-paddling the channel, then lazily floating back down the lovely Jade Pool.

DANGEROUS COURSE?

Yes, heaven is up around the bend. But how do you get there? Even in summer, the canyon above Ranger Hole is a steep channel of racing water. However, it also poses a very fun and exciting climbing course to test your courage and physical limits.

Most anyone can spider-crawl along the quarter-mile course in minutes. The secret is to stay to the bluffs on your right, where rock shelves with handholds will keep you high and dry. At the furthest bend, just beyond sight of Ranger Hole, will be the only point at which you might need to step into water. It might get thigh-deep for a few feet but you'll stay safe as long as you keep one hand on the ledge and your other gripping a walking stick in the stream to steady you.

Past the last cataract, the rapids taper off and the Duckabush runs quiet. Far ahead, you should see the jade-green glow and shining silver bluffs. You're in another world, with the roar of the rapids far behind you. Please give this place a chance to cast its spell on you.

Tip for Cheaters: A secondary trail will take you to the Jade Pool, completely avoiding the canyon rapids. Find the trail's branch just before you step out onto the cliffs above Ranger Hole.

From top: Lena Creek heavy flow at beginning of goat trail, right side; climbing a Hamma Hamma River log jam upstream from the Lena Creek Campground; winter trip to Upper Jorstad Falls.

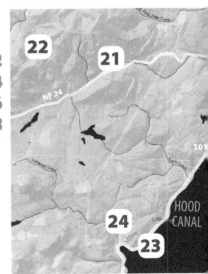

Hamma Hamma Watershed

8. Upper Hamma Hamma Falls 30
9. Lower Hamma Hamma Falls & Swimming Hole. 32
10. Beaver Pond Trail 34
11. Hamma Hamma Bottoms 35
12. Goat Trail above Lena Creek 36
13. Lena Creek Campground & River Access 37
14. Lena Lake 38
15. Cabin Creek Falls 40
16. The art of Canyoneering 42
17. Zip Line Canyon 44
18. Watson Creek Falls 46
19. Four Mile Falls 48
20. Waketickeh Creek 49

Jorstad - Lilliwaup

21. Upper Jorstad Falls 52
22. Washington Pass (FR #2441) . 54
23. Craig's Beach, Lilliwaup 56
24. Lilliwaup Falls 58

8/Upper Hamma Hamma Falls

DIRECTIONS
From Highway 101 north of Eldon, take the Hamma Hamma Recreation Area Road (FR #25). SET ODOMETER. At 6.4 miles you'll come to a "Y" with a bridge to your left. BEAR RIGHT instead, going 7.2 miles past Lena Creek Trailhead and Campground, to the falls.

SEASONAL CONCERNS	ROAD CONDITIONS	TRAIL DIFFICULTY	SAFETY CONCERNS	TRAILHEAD PASS?
SNOW LEVEL	4WD POTHOLES	SHORT BUT STEEP	CLIFFS KID CAUTION	FOREST PASS

Definitions of Terms: Pages 14-15

Upper Hamma Hamma Falls is a truly astounding site, especially for residents of the area who often come away from the falls, commenting, "I had no idea we had anything like that so close to Shelton," (or Belfair, or Union, etc.). While not the tallest, no other waterfall in Mason County is more dramatic and photo-inspiring. The surroundng scenery is five-star, too.

The unpaved forest road to the falls climbs gradually but tops out at nearly 2,000 feet. Approaching them is nearly impossible during winter due to snow level, for the road is not plowed. Summer the road is dry and dusty. Potholes and rain ruts are constant hazards on this road, which means that during rainy springs and autumns, you'll be bouncing down about 6 miles of "rough country" after the pavement ends just beyond the bridge over Lena Creek.

I highly recommend only 4WD vehicles attempt this road, except for adventurers who want to roll the dice in summer, when it might be passable for regular cars.

DESCRIPTION
Upper Hamma Hamma Falls are located at the end of Forest Road #25, which is also the trailhead for Mildred Lakes in the Mount Skokomish Wilderness. At the trailhead you'll find a pit toilet and a single picnic table.

A large and formidable concrete bridge dominates the area. It crosses above the falls, providing a viewing perch directly over the two-tiered beauty. Straight ahead, a line of jagged mountains will take your breath away.

The main plunge, about 100 feet, roars straight down from a cliff edge, not against a verticle rock face, like Murhut and Rocky Brook. This is a sheer drop, with a foaming, swirling gyre pulsing in a deep, dark pool below. Sculpted cliffs frame the falls on both sides, providing risky but breathtaking, amazing perches to view the falls from above.

An equally impressive upper tier plunges about 35 feet into an upper pool, forming a deep bowl directly below the bridge.

To experience the power of the falls from above them, take either of the pair of trails that start at the trailhead side of the bridge. They're dusty, loose-rock trails, so go slow and hold onto shrubs, branches and roots to ease your way down. The roar of the falls is awesome and it dominates all else. From the pool at the top of the upper plunge, you take a break, feel safe, and soak it all in.

If you bring kids, however, exercise extreme caution.

THE FALL MONTY

Getting a postcard photo of the face of the falls will require you to scramble down another dusty, loose trail. But this is the best view and well worth it.

Cross the bridge and walk nearly all the way back along the silver guardrail. Small cairns and a faint trail of white stones used to indicate the trailhead, but don't depend on these. Hop the guardrail near its end and look for a trail breaking the brush and leading down the very steep hill. Stay low and descend sideways, stairstepping with the side edges, not toes, of your shoes.

The trail ends at a high niche above the canyon, but with a monstrous, lovely view of the entire falls across the way. This is your reward and I guarantee it won't disappoint. Happy shooting!

Going off trail at Upper Hamma Hamma Falls will get you great views from across the canyon, but is a very dangerous venture above the falls itself.

9/Lower Hamma Hamma Falls & Swimming Hole

DIRECTIONS

Same directions as to Upper Hamma Hamma Falls. From the "Y" at the end of the Hamma Hamma Road (FS #25), bear right and go about 5 miles or until you begin to see very large, bus-sized boulders on the left edge of the road. The third boulder will be the biggest. You come to it .2 miles after passing a very tall, exposed cliff on your right. A lone mile marker sign is just before the trail. Look for pullout parking spots and a tree leaning against the left side of the boulder. A short but steep trail begins just before this largest boulder, dropping straight down to the pool and falls.

SEASONAL CONCERNS	ROAD CONDITIONS	TRAIL DIFFICULTY	SAFETY CONCERNS	TRAILHEAD PASS?
SNOW LEVEL	4WD POTHOLES	EASY	MILD KID CAUTION	NONE

Definitions of Terms: Pages 14-15

Lower Hamma Hamma Falls is not on the map--yet. But I promise you, once you visit this place, you will never forget it.

It's on the way to the upper falls, and I usually go there on my return, after seeing the big, monstrous upper falls first. This isn't a place of overwhelming power, but rather, an oasis of astounding natural beauty. If you could apply the term "Shangri La" to one location in Mason County, this is probably it. And while only the most radical outdoors enthusiasts will perch from the 100-foot bluffs of the upper falls to "hang out," the lower falls and swimming hole are exactly the kind of place that most anybody will want to bring a picnic basket, blankets, towels, kids, and maybe a snorkel mask and fins to, too.

Stick around, 'cause there's lots to do.

WHAT'S IT LIKE?

Think of a jigsaw and how it cuts a zigzag pattern. The lower falls are a pair of jigsaws, cutting parallel channels through sheer rock, over 25 feet thick. Then the channels meet, where, if you observe closely, one falls has cut through with such power that the water shoots below solid rock, then rushes back up from the other side.

You have to see it for yourself. A very brave diver, with a good safety line, might be able to drop in the upper chute and come back out below. Who knows.

And while the fabulous "S" curves of the falls are phenomenal to study, scramble, and hang out upon, it's the otherworldly swimming hole, with its torquise blue water so clear that you can read the date on a submerged quarter--the main pool is near 20 feet deep--anyway, it's the swimming hole that makes this place so lovely, and so beloved.

Now, this is one of the colder places in the Olympics to swim. No doubt. The way I approach it is: one full dip, as quick as possible, and then, without screaming or showing your audience too much pain, ease out of the water, knowing you have, most likely, just achieved a "personal best" for enduring the coldest water you are likely to survive in your entire life.

Wrap yourself in a warm towel of victory.

The cliffs and rocks around the main pool allow all kinds of sun bathing and ways to get in and out of the water safely. This place is totally suitable for romantic picnics, children, and offers hours of recreation and exploration options, both upstream and down.

BUDDHA VERSUS SPRING BREAK

Now, this is also the kind of place that will be abused as a "party spot." If you are reading these words now, please make a pledge that you will only come here to *worship* nature, not to ruin her.

Pick up any litter you may see, and take care to stay on existing trails, never cut wood or build fires on the ledges.

10/Beaver Pond Trail

DIRECTIONS

Same as to Hamma Hamma Falls. Set your ODOMETER at the Lena Creek Bridge, just after passing Lena Creek Campground. Beaver Pond is 1.6 miles beyond the bridge, marked by a little brown sign on the left.

SEASONAL CONCERNS	ROAD CONDITIONS	TRAIL DIFFICULTY	SAFETY CONCERNS	TRAILHEAD PASS?
SNOW LEVEL	4WD POTHOLES	EASY-MODERATE	SAFE	NONE

Definitions of Terms: Pages 14-15

Over the next seven chapters we'll be discovering little gems of beauty that are all located, or begin from, the same short stretch of the Hamma Hamma River. It's quite amazing how many accessible waterfalls, swimming holes, canyons, trails and scenic views are found so near each other.

You'll find the Beaver Pond Trail a couple miles before Lower Hamma Hamma Falls. The trailhead sign is so small many people drive right past it, never knowing a trail is there at all.

Now, this is not a "wild and crazy" kind of destination, but more of a meditation trail. It was established with help of the Audobon Society, so keep in mind that it's main attractions are birds.

THE TRAIL

The trail's length is just about a mile. After descending 200 feet of moderate decline (passing a lone tall boulder on the right which hides a shallow cave), you'll come to the viewing bench where the path diverges left and right to circle the Beaver Pond.

I like to loop the pond counter-clockwise. The trail itself is fun to follow, passing around one of the largest old growth stumps in the Olympics, and, at the far end of the pond, the trail squeezes among a forest of snarly vine maple--great weird tree photos! Mattress-deep moss beds, sunken logs around the pond's edge, resting benches and fine, creative trail work make your visit worthwhile.

However, the water table gets high here, with the river too high to take this trail in the rainy season. It's best for summer and autumn hikes.

Mountain view looking northwest over the Beaver Pond.

11/Hamma Hamma Bottoms

DIRECTIONS

Same as to Hamma Hamma Falls. Set your ODOMETER at the Lena Creek Bridge, just after passing Lena Creek Campground. Go another .4 miles and bushwhack left toward the river.

SEASONAL CONCERNS	ROAD CONDITIONS	TRAIL DIFFICULTY	SAFETY CONCERNS	TRAILHEAD PASS?
HIGH WATER	DECENT ROAD	EASY (NO TRAIL)	SAFE	NONE

Definitions of Terms: Pages 14-15

Whereas the Beaver Pond Trail is a perfectly scripted walk, the Hamma Hamma Bottoms are a dense, wild maple forest, noted for its tall, moss-sleeved trees, network of dry, gravel bed channels and rotted deadfall logs that collapse beneath your weight.

No official trails cross this floodplain. What human and animal trails you may find will prove to be hard to follow; this place is virtually made for you to get lost in, the very opposite of a "walk in the park."

Seriously, this place is perfect for learning wayfinding skills. You're never out of earshot of the river (west), with the opposite way leading you back to your car on the road (east).

However, in between those two, you'll find a deep, mysterious forest like no other in this part of the Olympics. This is a high valley floodplain with rocky soil, constantly disturbed by seasonal floods. Logged long ago, the Bottoms were never replanted with fir. Massive, gnarly maple trees took over, and a whole ecosystem has evolved with them.

Way back toward the river is an outlaw hideout, well hidden and used for campfires long after burn bans go into effect. Don't confront anyone you meet here. Unfortunately, this campsite is very near a set of beautiful rapids and a spectacular old growth log bridge.

Visit here April through October. Use the dry river channels as your main routes for getting around. Prepare to bushwhack when losing your trail.

Twisted branches, wrapped in moss, wait for visitors to the Hamma Hamma Bottoms, where hardwood trees dominate the canopy.

12/Goat Trail above Lena Creek

DIRECTIONS
Same as to Hamma Hamma Falls. Bear right at the "Y" and go 1.6 miles to Lena Creek Bridge. The goat trail starts behind the right-side campsite just BEFORE the bridge.

SEASONAL CONCERNS	ROAD CONDITIONS	TRAIL DIFFICULTY	SAFETY CONCERNS	TRAILHEAD PASS?
ALL SEASON	DECENT ROAD	MODERATE-DIFFICULT	CLIFFS KID CAUTION	NONE

Definitions of Terms: Pages 14-15

A pair of amazingly scenic trails can be found on both sides of the Lena Creek Bridge. Lena Creek is the wild, tumbling waterway that hikers hear as they zigzag up the Lena Lake Trail. Flowing from the lake, the creek pours into the Hamma Hamma River after flowing beneath the bridge.

Several choice campsites bracket the Lena Creek Bridge; in summer they are often full for days at time.

What's so special about these trails? Both give glimpses into one of the steepest, wildest canyons anywhere in the Olympics. From the upper goat trail, which follows the canyon rim and is dangerously high, you can see the craggy course of Lena Creek as she roars over several 100-foot cascades, her white turbulence fanning from boulder to boulder. Unfortunately, thick trees make for photo frustration.

TRAIL LOCATIONS
Find the lower unmarked trailhead on your right immediately after crossing the bridge (park on the road shoulder). The trail follows Lena Creek on its left flank and ends shortly where the canyon wall prevents any further progress, though determined scramblers can press on. It features nice places to camp or simply hang out while you admire the rapids.

A separate goat trail is found beyond the campsite on the right side just BEFORE the bridge. It, too, follows the creek, but climbs to a series of overlooks that gain in height. The trail winds ever higher, often without handholds over sections of loose rock--with still more tantalizing glimpses of waterfalls far up the canyon.

This trail requires full attention and is not recommended for small children. With dangerous cliffs and rapid elevation gain, it is a short, wild, cardio workout, taking you 500 feet above the rocky canyon below.

13/Hamma Hamma River Access: Lena Creek Campground

DIRECTIONS

Right at the "Y" at the end of the Hamma Hamma Recreation Road, go about 1.5 miles, passing Lena Lake Trailhead just before the campground, on your left.

SEASONAL CONCERNS	ROAD CONDITIONS	TRAIL DIFFICULTY	SAFETY CONCERNS	TRAILHEAD PASS?
HIGH WATER	DECENT ROAD	CANYON	WATER CROSSINGS	NONE AT RESTROOM

*Definitions of Terms: Pages 14-15

You absolutely must try this when the weather gets hot. Pull into the Lena Creek Campground (open seasonally) and park at the rest rooms or near the campground self-register kiosk.

Better yet, pack for a few nights and reserve Campsite #4, which features your very own fallen old growth cedar, with a towering root ball that kids will climb for hours.

From the campsite or via tiny trails leading from the register kiosk, head toward the sound of the flowing river. Typically, by the end of July the water flow ought to be low enough for "river running," a super-fun family sport of the highest calibre.

Here, and for a full mile upstream, the Hamma Hamma winds lazily, making "S" curves between high banks of sun-warmed river stones. Amazingly, she pools into deep eddies, or fans wide, breaking into knee-high riffles that you can cross safely, provided you use a walking stick and hold loved ones' hands.

Pack lunches into day packs and bring plenty of sunscreen. The riverbank beaches bake in the sun, totally fine for bikinis. This is a super grand time and other locals know of this incredible sport. Follow the river up and down, treasure hunting along its rocky banks, and be prepared to cross massive driftwood piles, again, using common sense and caution.

The moving river is cold. No downplaying that. But on a hot day, the 360-degree mountain scenery, blue skies, and clear blue water will help you overcome your shyness--you may find yourself indulging in cold plunges all day long.

If you've never dipped in a Northwest river, this is the one place to do it, and never forget the experience!

14/Lena Lake Trail

DIRECTIONS

Highway 101, go north of Hoodsport. Left onto Hamma Hamma Recreation Road, 6.4 miles to the "Y," bear right, going about a mile to Lena Lake Trailhead.

SEASONAL CONCERNS	ROAD CONDITIONS	TRAIL DIFFICULTY	SAFETY CONCERNS	TRAILHEAD PASS?
SNOW LEVEL	DECENT ROAD	LONG MODERATE	PICNIC SAFE	FOREST PASS

Definitions of Terms: Pages 14-15

Lena Lake has a great reputation and is probably the Number One trailhead, in terms of annual number of visitors, in Mason County's portion of the Olympic National Forest.

Drawing a constant crowd from Seattle and Olympia, on summer weekends you might find as many as 60 cars parked at the trailhead.

Lena has good reasons for her popularity. After a moderate, steady climb of 1,200 feet in three miles, you can pitch your tent and cook over a fire beside an Olympic Mountain lake, enjoying a genuine wilderness experience that is far removed from the madness of the modern world.

If you time it right, you can see the Northern Lights from here. Or stars reflecting in her glass-still, darkened waters.

For the first two miles or so, Lena Lake Trail is a no-nonsense, well maintained, switchback-after-switchback ascent to a well-deserved resting area in an upper basin. Here, a magnificent, rustic footbridge stands among an ancient tumble of boulders, the result of a long-ago landslide that collapsed part of the mountain and pinched off Lena Lake—a process similar to nearby Jefferson Lake, by the way, which was formed from a landslide triggered by an earthquake.

Lena Creek runs through the boulder gulley, coursing underground during summer and early autumn months. When she re-emerges, spurting out of the hillside, the creek flows down through one of the Olympic Peninsula's most spectacular, dramatic gorges, still roaring and tumbling white where she can be seen from the Lena Creek Bridge, a short distance past the trailhead, before finally merging with the Hamma Hamma River.

The gorge is immensely steep and dangerous and not developed for foot traffic at the present time. You can hear Lena Creek's many waterfalls and cataracts as you climb the switchbacks of the Lena Lake Trail.

THE LAKE, AND BEYOND

Lena Lake boasts 28 campsites with metal fire rings, plus a vault toilet that works overtime due to popular demand. The lake gets warm enough (barely, to make a pun) for swimming in summer, and is simply a great meditation partner, year-round, with her ring of tall trees, rocks to sit and picnic on, and mountain vistas to the north and west.

Two trails branch off from the lake's far end. One goes to Upper Lena Lake, a true alpine lake above 4,500 feet in Olympic National Park. You must earn this prize with a serious, steep climb.

The second trail is the access route to towering 6,842-foot The Brothers. After a couple of miles, the trail turns into a steep, rocky ascent of the peak, which is rated a technical climb for experienced mountaineers only, equipped with proper climbing gear.

However, about a mile from Lena Lake, the trail to The Brothers passes through a deep, pristine and near-prehistoric valley, an ancient forest of giant trees, boulders, and vast lands carpeted in the deepest moss. It has been nicknamed "The Valley of the Silent Men" for it's eerie, jaw-dropping scenery that will stun you into speechlessness and, as a second legend has it, for sleepy-headed Boy Scouts who had to break camp early at Lena Lake and then march through the Valley on their way to The Brothers.

Either way, if you can make it to Lena Lake, you owe it to yourself to hike a little further into the Valley of the Silent Men. It's Mother Nature's unforgetable gift simply waiting for you. With the Northwest's long summer days, a trip to the Valley and back makes a perfect, challenging day hike, including lunch and a brisk swim at lovely Lena Lake.

15/Cabin Creek Falls

DIRECTIONS

From Highway 101, turn onto Hamma Hamma Road, go 6.4 miles to the "Y," bear right, going about a half-mile to a gated road on your right. Park and proceed on foot the length of the road, to where it opens upon a large clearing. Bear very slightly to your left and follow the gentle rise toward the far end of the clearing. You must poke around at the forest's edge to find the remaining path. Stay on that path to the end, about 800 yards, moving toward the sound of Cabin Creek. The trail drops to the right and follows along the bluff above the creek, bringing you to the upper falls, where you drop down, cross the creek and continue downstream to the otterfalls, sunny picnic ledge, and 20-foot lower falls.

SEASONAL CONCERNS	ROAD CONDITIONS	TRAIL DIFFICULTY	SAFETY CONCERNS	TRAILHEAD PASS?
HIGH WATER	DECENT ROAD	EASY UNTIL THE END	PICNIC SAFE	NONE

Definitions of Terms: Pages 14-15

Forget Great Wolf Lodge and all those expensive, chlorinated water slides! Cabin Creek Falls is a gorgeous, wild location that fully functions as a safe, envigorating water park for kids. For first-time creek dippers, I guarantee you will find this to be a heavenly spot, especially when summertime temperatures poke into the 80s and higher.

Clear, cool water runs year-round from the mountain highlands surrounding Lena Lake. Cabin Creek drops into the Hamma Hamma Valley, where it streams around a tall, massive boulder, dropping over giant logs trapped between the boulder and a rock shelf, spilling into the first of several swimming holes.

For the next 200 yards, Cabin Creek zigzags between rocks and ledges, pouring round and over a natural obstacle course of knee-high rapids and water-worn channels. When summer flows are just right, the creek runs low enough to create an amazing series of kid-sized otterfalls, or, what I like to call Mother Nature's Chutes and Ladders.

ADVENTURERS ONLY

This place is made for the adventurous. If you bring children, I think six might be the minimum age (without close, hands-on supervision) and they should be children who are used to outdoor play, tree climbing, running around a farm, etc. This is for kids who like to jump, climb, roll and swim.

Dads will love conquering the otterfalls with excited kids squealling and holding their hands.

A huge flat stone ledge nestles beside the second and largest of three waterfalls, towering over a 20-foot drop. Excellent for sunning, watching small babies, and unpacking picnics, you can spread your towels here and soak up rays between cool dips. Below the ledge, another tall boulder rises from the middle of the creek. It can be climbed, as well as a rock wall leading back up to the picnic ledge.

The water is deep but narrow below the second falls, and I cannot say with certainty that sport jumping is possible here. A smaller falls pours into a final, wide shallow pool. The view upstream from here is astounding. Actually, every step you take at Cabin Creek Falls opens to a scenic, fantastic world.

I will be blamed terribly for publicizing this five-star sacred spot. I do believe it can stand up to foot traffic, however, and my higher hopes are that greater awareness of such places will inspire additional resources to go towards more facilities and better management of Olympic National Forest.

Lower Cabin Creek Falls with picnic ledge on right.

16/The Art of Canyoneering

Hey, momma, I want a new watersport!

I'm hoping one of the byproducts of this book will be your greater interest in the sport of canyoneering. Hugely popular in the desert Southwest, where many canyons form deep, dry roads that can be walked for miles, Northwest canyoneering remains a decidedly wetter and more demanding version of the sport.

Still, with climate change bringing longer summer droughts to the Pacific Northwest, many rivers of the Olympic Peninsula now run low enough to be navigable to anyone with a little grit and a walking stick.

A walking stick is a MUST. With it, you master what I call the Triangle of Traction.

On the contrary, if you misjudge one slick rock without the support of your trusty stick, your canyon trip is over faster than you can say bruises and contusions.

Setting that warning aside, I can't wait for more people to catch the passion of canyoneering. The main reason there are so many fantastic places included in *Where the Waterfalls and Wild Things Are* is that, by and large, I use streams and rivers as my trails. I've discovered a whole new trail network, as a matter of fact, with so many waterways leading to water*falls*.

If your stick is your essential vehicle of travel, then your essential *method* of travel is the art of rock hopping.

Children are naturally good at this; it's why balancing on the curb of a street can be so compelling to them. Essentially, as you move up and down the banks of a river or stream, you encounter rocks. Rocks of all sizes.

Armed with pliable rubber soles (sandals, tennis shoes or any of the "river wear" hybrids), you progress up and downstream by stepping from one rock to the next. Over long lengths, when the canyon runs level, there's no other way to go. Whether conscious or not, careful or not, you are presented with a vast mosaic of individual rocks.

Nature is now conducting a personality test. If the rock-by-rock form of travel irritates or bugs you, then you will, most likely, not fall in love with canyoneering.

For, in addition to small-rock sections of tedius travel, canyoneering-- especially creek canyoneering--will often present you with sections of boulders, or even waterfalls, to get over. Here you must climb, scramble, pull up, crawl across, toss gear, wade through, and sometimes *jump in* cold, moving water to advance at all.

Obviously, this, too, will likely thin the ranks of would-be canyoneer aficionados.

It's best to be honest about the challenge and occasional difficulties of canyoneering.

But my gosh, once you actually get up into a place like Washington Creek, Cabin Creek Falls, or down the magnificent Skokomish, you will soften your focus in regards to potential dangers. Rather, you will be charmed, mystified-- dare I say "swept away"--by the power, beauty and speechless spirituality of being a lone human being keenly alive, exploring step by step, rock by rock, in and out of moving, sacred water.

Caves. Cliffs. Blue jewel pools. Silver braids of waterfalls, tumbling cotton cataracts. And oh, the warm slab of rock, welcome as a smooth cheek to kiss, where you unload your pack and make a pillow of it, lying back to watch the sun darting behind tall maples or sparkling gold on the stream beside you.

Every creek and river has a story to tell. Some, like the Skokomish, shout messages of awe from deep in her 500-foot canyons. Some simply whisper like Waketickeh, Murhut, Jorstad and Jefferson Creek. Some tell stories, and others, like Watson Creek, open you to silence and no stories at all.

Canyoneering leads to an intense, moment by moment understanding of the world. The intensity of walking and watching your balance for long periods of time, rock by rock, step by step, drills down to an inner mantra.

This is a sport of immersion. As you immerse, accept, and become one with your challenges, you can learn to let go of judgments. You now approach a place long forgotten: the balancing games of your childhood, hill rolling, tumbling, pillow-fighting. Tangling with the monsters under your bed. And at the same time, you move into a very open, welcoming space full of newness, creativity and positivity.

Thus the fabulous picnic on the rock overlooking the canyon. The wine among friends skinny dipping in the sunny stream. The indescribable lovemaking on the ledge behind the waterfall.

You're Captain Kirk on a brand new planet, exploring new worlds that can't help but enlarge your own.

17/Zip Line Canyon

DIRECTIONS
From Highway 101, turn onto Hamma Hamma Recreation Road, go 6.4 miles to the "Y," and park on either side of the bridge visible on your left.

SEASONAL CONCERNS	ROAD CONDITIONS	TRAIL DIFFICULTY	SAFETY CONCERNS	TRAILHEAD PASS?
HIGH WATER	DECENT ROAD	CANYON	SWIFT WATER	NONE

Definitions of Terms: Pages 14-15

Zip Line Canyon got its name from a thick strand of logging cable stretched tight between two trees along a bank above the Hamma Hamma River.

This is the thick, heavy duty cable they used on the old growth to wrestle them up the hills and drag them to the flatbed trucks. I imagine one day long ago, as the last of the big trees were cut and taken from this stretch of the river, the following idea came up between a few loggers on their last lunch break: let's wrap some cable around a maple down here on the bank, and string it across and up to another tree on the cliff above, about 20 feet higher.

Frankly, I don't know exactly who did it, or how long ago, but a circus tightrope of logging cable stretches high above the ground in a very dramatic section of canyon, both ends fully embedded in the flesh of both trees, the bark grown around them. (A ménage à trees?) The cable is strung as tight as a drum. When I last saw it three years ago, it had a long, thick yellow crust of dried moss along its entire length, like toothpaste on a brush, which told me nothing heavier than a bird had been on that cable for a long, long time.

Strong arms and good leather gloves would get you the First Human to Descend the Loggers Zip Line Award.

THE CANYON
Zip Line Canyon is visible all year long. Its lower entrance begins at the "six mile" Hamma Hamma Bridge, the one to your left when you reach the "Y" at the end of the Hamma Hamma Recreation Area Road (FS #25).

This trip is recommended for August and September, when the river is at its lowest. Basically, if you're standing on the six mile bridge and looking up river and the rapids are white, frothy and coursing over rocks with speed, it means the water is too high to maneuver safely.

However, if you see lots of exposed rocks and only a tiny bit of white water at the farthest point upstream, then the river is ready for walking.

Grab your stick and start upsteam, hugging the left bank, or wading in and out of the shallow pools along the left side. Eventually, when the bridge is almost out of view behind you, the rocks will get much larger and the canyon walls steeper.

Look for the Logger's Zip Line running from the cliff above. Soon after finding it, the ledge on the left grows too high to get around. This is a "Pinch," a point in a canyon where you must either (a) stop; (b) go back and climb around; or (c) ford the river to continue upstream.

Try fording. Even with low water, you are liable to get wet here, but it is a fun maze of boulders and logjams, and full of places to wade, sunbathe and explore. Another 100 yards upstream the entire river squeezes down to a narrow channel that you can literally hop over, staying dry.

Lazy person's shortcut: Look for the faint trail going up the bank on the right side. That's your fast exit from the canyon. You'll come to the road about two-tenths of a mile beyond the bridge. Obviously, you can start your canyon trip from here.

Extreme low water in the Hamma Hmma makes it possible to canyoneer your way upstream from the six mile bridge.

18/Watson Falls

DIRECTIONS

At 5.5 miles on Hamma Hamma Road, park below the steep drive to the Hamma Hamma Cabin. Further directions in chapter text.

SEASONAL CONCERNS	ROAD CONDITIONS	TRAIL DIFFICULTY	SAFETY CONCERNS	TRAILHEAD PASS?
FALLS DIMINISH	DECENT ROAD	LOWER: EASY UP: CANYON	MILD KID CAUTION	NONE

Definitions of Terms: Pages 14-15

I highly, highly recommend Watson Falls to the beginning canyoneerer. Watson has two distinct falls, the lower at the end of a short, easy trail, and the upper after a short bushwack over some boulders and logs. This is kid-friendly fun, with the upper falls tumbling beside a shallow cave, and with enough sunny river rocks around to work up a beach picnic, Olympic rainforest-style.

Visit in April, May, June. Watson Creek often goes dry by July.

WHERE TO?

Five-and-a-half miles up the Hamma Hamma Road you'll see the small sign and turnoff for historic Hamma Hamma Cabin (which you can rent, by the way) on your right. Without blocking it, park at the bottom of the drive. Grab your sticks, your lunch and other goodies, and walk up the gated drive or, as an alternative, walk back down the road toward Highway 101. After a few hundred feet, you'll see the crosswalk and pathways for the Living Legacy Trail.

Take the left (north and uphill) path which follows Watson Creek on your right. A few hundred yards of gentle rise and you'll crest near a bench and historic interpretive sign. Head away from the creek and toward the red cabin. As you near the cabin, look for a faint trail bearing to the right. It may be partially obscured at first, but this trail opens up and should be easy to follow. You'll note beautiful moss beds and woods all around.

After a quarter mile the trail steepens near its end and you should hear the falls roaring louder. Just before you see the falls, you'll come to a large, gurgling cistern--a big plastic keg--holding fresh-piped water. This untreated water pipes downhill to the taps at the cabin. I drink from here. But I am not telling you to do it, okay?

Welcome to Lower Watson Falls, famous for its signature "V" shape and, at one time, a log that leaned far over its 25-foot height that would allow you to sit on its end, posing for great--if not somewhat dangerous-- photos. Here, you'll also appreciate the flat, level viewing spot that also makes a nice picnic circle for those who don't want to continue to the upper falls.

UPPER FALLS

Follow the trail that hugs the ledge on your left. Look for a way down to the stream bed just above the lip of the falls. (At one time marked by a rope.) It's fun to hang out here, and maybe that log still juts over the falls' edge.

Head upstream, climbing the large boulder, and be ready to scramble over many more rocks, logs and snarled tree roots to reach Upper Watson Falls--a very short, yet a-maze-ing bushwhack. Here, in the narrowest of canyons, Upper Watson is a sweet, sinewy tumbler that braids her way down a mossy cliff face, splashing into a dark, cold pool partially hidden beneath a cave-like ledge.

At high noon on hot days, I believe this spot gets enough sun to make it a worthy picnic or cold dip destination. The "Northwest Wild" view of the mossy cliffs towering a hundred feet above the falls-- that alone makes this spot special.

High winter flow at Lower Watson Falls, found at the end of a short, easy trail beginning at the Hamma Hamma Cabin.

20/Four Mile Falls

DIRECTIONS
Exactly four miles west on the Hamma Hamma Recreation Area Road. Look right.

SEASONAL CONCERNS	ROAD CONDITIONS	TRAIL DIFFICULTY	SAFETY CONCERNS	TRAILHEAD PASS?
FALLS RUN DRY	DECENT ROAD	EASY	SAFE	NONE

*Definitions of Terms: Pages 14-15

This is the Goldilocks "just right" waterfall, not too big, not too small, and surprisingly hidden in plain sight exactly four miles in on the Hamma Hamma Road. Thus the name Four Mile Falls.

There's barely enough road shoulder to park on when you see the falls, a fantail white strip on your right as you drive westward. Look for the large rocks on your right shortly after passing the pink concrete wall.

The falls are barely 100 yards from the road and you'll pick up the trail immediatey after leaving your car. Several little way trails angle off to points along the creek, and these make fine places from which to photograph the falls.

The falls slide about 30 feet from their topmost point, spreading wider like a fan as they pour over a jutting brow of mossy rock. They spill into a knee-high pool perfect for small children in the summer. The falls form a

peaceful, serene setting which is all the more special for being so near the road.

If you stand back and observe closely, the falls add another 10 feet in height with a sepatate chute of turgid water spilling into a bowl before tumbling the final 30 feet.

Four Mile Falls, beautiful to photograph when dusted with winter snow, will go completely dry most every summer.

Hidden in plain sight, modest (and sometimes dry) Four Mile Falls tumbles right beside the Hamma Hamma Recreation Area Road.

21/Waketickeh Creek

DIRECTIONS
From Highway 101, turn onto the Hamma Hamma Recreation Area Road, driving exactly 2.4 miles to the bridge crossing Waketickeh Creek.

SEASONAL CONCERNS	ROAD CONDITIONS	TRAIL DIFFICULTY	SAFETY CONCERNS	TRAILHEAD PASS?
FALLS DIMINISH	DECENT ROAD	CANYON	WATER CROSSINGS	NONE

*Definitions of Terms: Pages 14-15

You don't have to go far at all to plunge into a premier canyoneering experience. Just 2.4 miles up the Hamma Hamma Road, to be exact, and you'll come to the concrete bridge crossing little Waketickeh Creek.

Waketickeh provides a special kind of journey, and was my first real venture into creek and canyon exploration, many years ago. I try to revisit Waketickeh every year.

Your visit should be on any warm day May through September, depending on creek level. Too little water is better than too much, as there is no trail of any kind, just a patient, slow progress up (or down) a deep forest Olympic riparian zone.

Park about 100 yards past the bridge, where another logging road turns sharply right.

Grab your gear, your stick, a lunch and a towel. This is going to be fun.

Below the bridge, look for any breaks in the brush and work your way down to the creek, heading upstream. Waketickeh should be gently bubbling, with riffles like little white teeth, but not be pushing hard against your legs when you get in. You should see plenty of dry rocks lining both banks and it should appear to be knee-deep or less for most of her visible length.

UPSTREAM PARADISE
This is the perfect creek for first-time canyoneers. You are going to be walking a mile or so, hopefully at a slow, leisurely pace, stepping from dry rock to dry rock, or learning how to "wet walk" straight up the stream. At times you must get around a log jam. You will need to crawl over, under, or around stacks of downed trees crossing the creek. Or over a single log spanning your way.

This is kid-friendly, family fun. Fairly soon you'll become immune to cold water; my daughter-in-law once did a very long stretch in bare feet, using a walking stick, of course.

You'll pass several little "party pools" along the way, beautiful eddies or sheltering shapes where you will want to linger. Sure, go ahead, grab a rest and a drink of water.

However, the spot you want to look for is a stretch of bare, solid rock where the creek runs against it like a chute on a waterslide. This is a fun "otterfall" place with gurgling riffles and worn bowl-shapes holding water, but the best place of all is just upstream.

After about 90 minutes (fast pace), you'll reach a lovely, calm swimming hole marked by a genteel, 10-foot waterfall with a sweet, rocky beach on your left--perfect for towels, discarded clothing, picnic food, and all the indulgences you can imagine and carry.

Welcome to one of the finest, most pristine swimming holes anywhere in the Olympics, a Northwest postcard proclaiming beauty: the moss, the ferns, the white bark of alders, the constant white of the falls churning musically. The short cliffs are perfect for jumping, even shallow diving, provided you know what you're doing. The pool depth is about five to seven feet. And while it's not Hawaiian hot, the water here will be most welcome after your vigorous, excitement-filled journey.

I've gone another half-mile further upstream, and it, too, is filled with wonders and beauty. The Waketickeh leads on, with another set of falls still waiting to be discovered, I believe.

DOWNSTREAM HEAVEN

Going downstream from the Waketickeh bridge is a pretty nice journey, too. It is a bit narrower going this way, with steep banks, yet not

as deep, overall, as the upper canyon.

Here, too, you'll come across some very sweet and appealing party pools, but the main goal will (again) be another spot where the creek runs in a shallow chute just below a heavenly wading pool, then tumbles, straight down, into a deep, calm channel.

Instead of viewing a falls, this time you're on top the falls.

You can't climb around. Both sides are too steep for getting past this obstacle, and it will seem that you can go no further without having to jump in, then swim, to the next dry spot in the creek.

That, in fact, is what I did. The water level was such that the falls were about seven feet above the deep channel. I left my gear back on top, and jumped in. Thankfully, I was able to climb alongside the tiny falls and pull myself back up.

If you have cameras and other gear, you will need a waterproof duffel to continue on this journey. The channel runs about 15 feet deep for a length of 100 feet or so. You have to jump in with your waterproof gear. But because of the sun-baked course the water follows above, the channel is not too cold here at all.

After coming out on the other end of the channel, the overall gorge gets deeper and more dramatic, with a section of otterfalls marked by several hot-tub-sized rock bowl indentions filled with warmer-than-normal water.

You will love this mini water park, on par with the waterslides at Cabin Creek Falls.

EXPEDITION THEORY

If you depart early enough on a June or July morning, my theory is that you can park one car on the road shoulder where Waketickeh Creek runs into Hood Canal north of Eldon, then drive another car to the bridge up the Hamma Hamma Road, where you park, debark and start your canyoneering journey downstream, arriving at Highway 101 before the sun goes down.

I have not made it this far myself, due to all the time I spent playing back at the otterslides and the falls. If there is a totally impassable falls or other obstacle below where I stopped exploring, I cannot say.

Whoever attempts this, however--and succeeds--would be the first.

My waterproof hat off to them!

21/Upper Jorstad Falls

DIRECTIONS

On Highway 101, go north 6 miles past Lilliwaup to Jorsted Creek Road, also known as Forest Service Road #24. Set your odometer after turning onto FS #24. It is exactly 4.8 miles to where you'll park and find the falls. Stay on FS 24, bearing left under the power lines at 2.2 miles, continuing until you see a white post with an "X" carved at the top at 4.6 miles. It is .2 miles before off-shoulder parking (marked with orange tree tape) on the right side of the road. Listen for the falls. The seldom-used trail goes to the creek then follows it upstream another 100 yards to the falls.

SEASONAL CONCERNS	ROAD CONDITIONS	TRAIL DIFFICULTY	SAFETY CONCERNS	TRAILHEAD PASS?
FALLS DIMINISH	POTHOLES	EASY	PICNIC SAFE	NONE

Definitions of Terms: Pages 14-15

Jorstad (sometimes spelled Jorsted) Creek, which flows into Hood Canal a mile south of the Hamma Hamma, boasts two unique and separate waterfalls, a 20-foot lower plunge that spreads wide over a rocky dome. The lower falls are by far the more beautiful and worthy of visits. Easy to admire from a hillside that is higher and opposite them, you can instantly see that they form a sheltered grotto below their splash, which makes a great, natural waterpark for kids to wade in and explore.

The rock slab forming the upper edge of the falls--when the water level is low--becomes a very cool place to hang out, picnic, or sun bathe. The right side of the ledge slants down, making for easy access between the top and bottom of the falls. Once, after shooting video of the sun darting through the tall tree canopy, I fell asleep on the upper ledge, after rolling up my jacket for a pillow.

NOT THIS TIME

Now, the bad news about the lower falls is that I am not providing directions to them. They lie nestled in a pristine and very fragile environment, a place where additional human traffic can produce none other than negative consequences.

There are a handful of places in the southeastern Olympics that also deserve this same protection, including another pair of waterfalls and several national forest campsites. Too many people will ruin them. Chapter 58, "The Waterfall Witness Protection Program" helps explain my thinking on this matter while allowing for a way that readers who choose to, might yet be part of the solution, not the problem.

UPPER FALLS

Upper Jorstad Falls are not as fragile as the lower one. Still, the irony is that recently the forested hill to the immediate left of the upper falls was clear cut, providing proof of how easily certain logging practices--mainly riparian rape--can endanger our fragile ecosystem.

Well before the recent clearcut, the steep gulley formed by Jorstad Creek, in which the upper falls lie, has been a collecting point for many fallen trees, principally pencil-like young alders, which tumble into the narrow chasm of the falls and lodge there, obstructing your view.

Today, the base of the falls reminds me of an artist's pencil cup.

Looking towards the future, that same phenomenon of fallen trees choking the riparian zone increases dramatically, thanks to the few remaining trees having no wind protection because their fellow "buffer" trees have been harvested.

Still, the upper falls are worth a visit, particularly if you are a waterfall collector.

You have to get close to the falls to really appreciate them. She has three visible drops: narrow, white braids, her final plunge of about 40 feet pelting the round, shallow pool at her bottom in a steady shower of drops. As she shrinks in the summer, water drips off ends of stringy green moss with just enough percussive play on the pool surface to cause maidenhair ferns growing along her rocky face to shimmer from the breeze.

The wading pool at her base is shallow, much like Four Mile Falls, and fine for small children to play in. Both falls' pools are dammed at their exits by smaller logs, sticks and debris that have fallen down and collected there. During a recent winter snow we visited the falls, much to our delight. Icicles, formed by her kickback spray, hung from the many fallen trees resting against her face.

Best time to visit Upper Jorstad Falls is during spring. Nearby salmon berry buds are pink and fresh leaves push out their vibrant greens. The moss and ferns, too, glow their brightest while the falls run widest in March, April, May.

Deadfall pile, behind family, creates shallow pool at base of Upper Jorstad Falls.

22/Washington Pass

DIRECTIONS

(Same as to Upper Jorstad Falls.) On Highway 101, go north 6 miles past Lilliwaup to Jorsted Creek Road, also known as Forest Service Road #24. Set your odometer immediately, staying on FR #24, bearing left under the power lines at 2.2 miles, continuing until you see a white post with an "X" carved at the top at 4.6 miles. From here, it is a half-mile or so to FR #2441, which bears steeply to your right..

SEASONAL CONCERNS	ROAD CONDITIONS	TRAIL DIFFICULTY	SAFETY CONCERNS	TRAILHEAD PASS?
SNOW LEVEL	4WD	EASY	SAFE	NONE

Definitions of Terms: Pages 14-15

This is all about the view. If you want an expansive, panoramic view of Hood Canal, Mt. Rainier and the wide, flat lands of Puget Sound, *but you don't want to climb a difficult mountain to get it*, then Washington Pass is for you.

It's quite close to Upper Jorstad Falls, covered in the previous chapter.

Except for the driest days of summer, I would recommend you use a high clearance or four-wheel-drive vehicle to reach the pass. You can still make it with regular traction, but 4WD is preferred for most logging roads.

Basically, Washington Pass is a 1,800-foot ridge summit on Forest Service Road #2441 providing a nice parking and turnaround spot, with a gorgeous, jaw-dropping view that requires nothing but you to roll down your window to appreciate it.

You certainly may walk around. Indeed, this is a good spot to get out,

stretch, and catch the sunrise over Mt. Rainier, as well as swirling fog or long sunset shadows. You can see some logging evidence, of course, but also glimpses of Melbourne Lake, Dow Mountain, rolling foothill humps, and the logging road you came up on, a tiny ribbon far below.

Beyond the pass, your road continues on for miles, descending wildly as it follows Washington Creek all the way to where it joins FR #2401 just beyond Upper Elk Lake.

However, just beyond your view at the pass, FR #2441 juts off into sub-roads that branch both left and right. These climb even higher but prove to be very undependable for traction, even by tough, 4WD standards. Go ahead and explore, but be aware that you may encounter a spot or two where the only sensible driving choice is to back down a very steep incline, looking over your shoulder the entire time you descend--not a favorite pastime of mine, I assure you.

Anyway, enjoy the view. It takes only 7 minutes to drive to the summit from where you first pick up FR #2441. If you do continue on, be aware that the road gets rougher, with plenty of loose, falling rocks. It's about five scary miles with no guardrails and few places to turn around.

When you see little, round Upper Elk Lake on your right, rejoice. You are through the thickest and about to connect with a major logging road leading out of the mountains, FR #2401, heading right.

Photographers capture snow, Hood Canal and clouds at little known Washington Pass. Dependable 4WD is your ticket to breathtaking high country all along Forest Road #2441.

23/Craig's Beach in Lilliwaup

DIRECTIONS

On Highway 101, look for the signs and stairway just north of the Lilliwaup Bridge.

SEASONAL CONCERNS	ROAD CONDITIONS	TRAIL DIFFICULTY	SAFETY CONCERNS	TRAILHEAD PASS?
ALL SEASON	DECENT ROAD	EASY	PICNIC SAFE	DISCOVER PASS

Definitions of Terms: Pages 14-15

Craig's Beach is the unofficial name for a one-mile stretch of rocky beachfront hidden below the bluffs of Highway 101, just north of Lilliwaup.

It is state-owned land but not nearly as populated or patrolled as nearby state parks. Yes, you'll need your Discover Pass.

What makes Craig's Beach special is its sense of isolation; after descending a handful of stairs, you will drop below most of the highway noise while, at the same time, open yourself to an unobstructed one-mile-long panoramic view of Hood Canal and its opposite shore.

This is a popular spot for fishing when the chum run close to shore. It's also a decent place to get fresh oysters, though the largest selection (as well as size) are found during low tide at Menard's Landing, a Mason County park on the Tahuya Peninsula.

SWIM, SUN, READ, WINE

Craig's Beach is mainly for relaxing. Though very few spots are blessed with fine, soft sand, near the bluffs you can spread your blankets on level pebbles and call it "good" from there. I recommend you bring a yoga mat for softer padding.

In summer the beach gets plenty of sun, so think of this as a great place to read, eat chocolate and cheese, and drink Chardonnay. Swim? Yes. The water gets decently warm.

Kids will be entertained for hours, too, as there are plenty of unusual, colored rocks here, as well as smooth beach glass, driftwood and unusual washed-up treasures.

I made spice racks from salvaged wooden crates found here.

Look for weird pock marks in the boulders below the bluffs; these bubbles are from ancient volcanic eruptions.

At low tide you may walk the entire one-mile length of the beach; the far end has a path back up to the road.

In spring, check out the hillsides on the other side of the road from where you park. Stroll north of the old landslide to admire or harvest fresh watercress and wild mint. In summer, the bluffs are loaded with blackberries.

Left: Looking south toward Indian Point from Craig's Beach in Lilliwaup.
Above: Steps and marker at trailhead on Highway 101.

24/Lilliwaup Falls

DIRECTIONS

Take Highway 101 north of Hoodsport to Lilliwaup. Just after passing the Lilliwaup Store and Community Club on your left, bear left just before you come to the abandoned building and bridge over Lilliwaup Creek. Continue down this lane, passing several cabins and a beautiful American Craftsman home with a waterfall in the backyard. Drive another .3 miles or so, going VERY SLOWLY over the speed bump. Soon you will come to the end of the road, facing a tall timber gate. Park here if the gate is open. You may walk to the bridge and no further. You cannot get a view of the falls from here but you can hear them off to your left. Sorry, but I need to repeat: do not trespass beyond the bridge, thank you very much.

SEASONAL CONCERNS	ROAD CONDITIONS	TRAIL DIFFICULTY	SAFETY CONCERNS	TRAILHEAD PASS?
FALLS DIMINISH	PRIVATE DRIVE	EASY	UPPER: CLIFFS	NONE (PRIVATE)

Definitions of Terms: Pages 14-15

Lilliwaup Falls was the queen of all Olympic Mountain waterfalls for nearly a century after the first white explorers settled in Hood Canal in the early 1850s. A stunning and mystical sight, the falls poured almost directly into the Canal, their roar heard by ships sailing past Lilliwaup Bay.

On old Washington State highway maps you can still find Lilliwaup Falls indicated by the state park symbol of a tiny green tree. The falls were once a state park before being bought by a very rich private citizen in the 1950s--a most interesting, if not outright dubious, transaction.

Though I can't recount for you the exact line of ownership, they are still in private hands. The good news is that Lilliwaup Falls, all 350-plus feet of her upper and lower sections, while not impossible to visit, are available only for pre-approved tours.

Some of the best photos of the falls were black-and-whites from the early 20th Century, taken from the high bluff on her southern side. They show all four ribbony stages of the lower falls dropping 250 feet as they jigsaw through solid rock.

UPPER FALLS

The upper falls, while not as tall, are more primitive, powerful and magnificent. For one thing, their surroundings are more wild, with a deep, difficult chasm that leads to rapids, then shapely swimming holes, and just as suddenly, thunderous cataracts. The upper falls begin with a 25-foot plunge into a deep, shadowy pool, then the falls roll over a 10-foot ledge to drop and swirl around the most pristine elevated swimming hole--a veritable tea cup--before crashing over the last 70 feet of solid rocky brow, striking the bottom with such force as to shoot back up like a fountain.

I've been following a long, arduous (and secret) route to the upper falls for years, beginning when I first lived in Lilliwaup in 1991.

There's a quicker, easier way, but you need to be invited, then escorted there.

When the water level is just right, the "tea cup" at the top of the upper falls is deep enough to dive in, wide enough to swim laps across, then pause at the very lip of the falls, your arms over the edge, as though you were taking a break from swimming in a skyscraper's rooftop pool.

Several times I have gotten up to sit on this very edge, 70 feet above a nasty fall, and blocked the water flow with my legs and butt-bottom cheeks. I'd let the water in the pool rise about eight inches or so, literally cutting off the falls, then jump out of the way and watch a huge surge of water go roaring down the face of the falls.

Ah, kids these days. What can you do?

Author takes the plunge in the canyon between Upper and Lower Lilliwaup Falls.

LOWER FALLS

The lower falls are taller, much more narrow, and hard to photograph. When the sun is out the falls are either in deep shade or blasted by direct glare reflecting off rock on either side.

The pool at the bottom is nice for wading, and during summer and fall chum runs, the creek is often full of fish, which go darting and finning wildly past you. There's an old lawn below the falls which makes for a good viewing location. The soil has been churned up a bit from seasonal flooding, so it's more of a rocky walk now--a far cry from the 1950s when the lawn was perfectly manicured and held a pressure fountain that would geyser 200 feet high and, at night, be illuminated by colored spotlights.

The genius behind the spotlights also decided that the lower falls were "crooked," so he paid workers to cement the waterfall, straight across, at the top of the last beautiful tier. Imagine orthodontic braces on the neck of a swan. It looks ridiculously straight and artificial now, worse than a bad ride at a cheesy waterpark.

The original mansion still stands, with plenty of good views from there. Beside the house stands the Long Live the Kings salmon hatchery--a very forward and involved nonprofit striving to restore and maintain local native salmon runs.

I'LL BE DAMMED

Since the 1920s the upper falls have been tapped for hydroelectricity. Much work was done recently to bring the dam and generators up to date.

To protect their investment, the land owners have installed many surveillance cameras.

Once a year I try to schedule a visit to both the upper and lower falls, with sometimes a trip down the five-star canyon linking them both. If curiosity to see the falls is driving you absolutely mad, please read the chapter on "The Waterfall Witness Protection Program" to see if you would be interested in attending one of these (rather rare) tours as well.

Left: Lower falls showing concrete edge to straighten falls. Right: Winter flow of magnificent Upper Lilliwaup Falls hides a fairly large cave carved out of its base, just behind ledge in foreground.

From top: Ripe salmon berries bob near the campsite at Upper Jefferson Falls; beaver's handiwork around trunk on Washington Creek; the "pinch," an obstacle course for canyoneers moving up Washington Creek Canyon, ranked as one of the best.

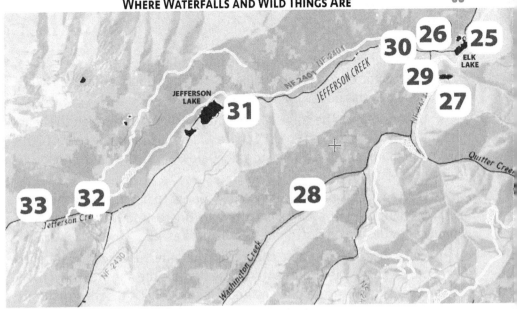

Jefferson Creek Watershed

25a. The 2018 Maple Fire....................64

25b. Elk Lake Trail..........................65

26. The Balds, Alternate Elk Lake Trail 66

27. Upper Elk Lake 69

28. Upper Washington Creek Swimming Hole..71

29. Washington Creek Swimming

      Hole & Canyon 74

30. Lower Jefferson Falls and campsites 76

31. Boulder Field - Jefferson Lake............78

32. Upper Jefferson Falls 82

33. Little Yosemite Valley...................86

25a/The 2018 Maple Fire

The Jefferson Creek watershed is home to many scenic, recreational treasures. Eight or more--including spectacular Upper Jefferson Falls--are detailed in this book.

Unfortunately, the tragic Maple Fire of 2018 raged through the heart of this forested area. The Forest Service will be spending the bulk of 2019 in road repairs and habitat restoration, closing off the entire region to visitors of any kind.

Limited access makes it impossible for me to update any conditions that pertain to your potential explorations. There is no way to accurately predict any destroyed restrooms, lost campsites, etc.

The subject of the first chapter in the Jefferson Creek Watershed section, Elk Lake, was at the center of the fire. It is the one area most likely to be very different from previous reports (even in 2020, when roads are expected to be reopened).

Trusting that Mother Nature will make a comeback from this type of fire, the best way to read the following eight chapters is to imagine a series of ideal destinations waiting for you.

In fact, the fire did not touch the shores of Jefferson Lake, or Little Yosemite and Upper Jefferson Falls, though you will not be able to visit those locations until October of 2019, at the earliest.

Again, the descriptions published in Chapters 25 through 33 are going to be incomplete and out-of-date due to the Maple Fire. I apologize and ask you to make allowance for that.

High water in early spring makes crossing the egress of Elk Lake nearly impossible. In summer you will cross a dry creek bed.

25b/Elk Lake Trail

DIRECTIONS

From Highway 101, take the Hamma Hamma Road (FS #25) to the "Y" at 6.4 miles. SET ODOMETER. Go left on Forest Road #2480 for 3 miles, then right on Forest Road #2401, which climbs immediately. Look for the Elk Lake Trailhead at 2.5 miles (5.5 odometer miles).

SEASONAL CONCERNS	ROAD CONDITIONS	TRAIL DIFFICULTY	SAFETY CONCERNS	TRAILHEAD PASS?
SNOW LEVEL	4WD	EASY	SAFE	FOREST PASS LOWER T.H.

Definitions of Terms: Pages 14-15

Elk Lake forms a shallow catch basin for Jefferson Creek snowmelt in normal years. Every spring it will typically swell to around 20 acres, and provide some fair fishing, as long as you are more appreciative of the scenery than the need to hook a big one.

Before the Maple Fire, the 2.5-mile loop trail around Elk Lake was always pleasant, nearly level--a perfect jogging trail as it followed the shore, passing under small stands of old growth timber.

Some very fine walk-in campsites dotted the southern shore. Nestled below protective old growth, the sites were secret treasures known only to locals.

The loop trail and campsites are normally accessed via the short but very steep road to the lake's egress point. This road is located on your right at about 2.5 miles from where you first pick up Forest Road #2401 at its junction with Forest Road #2480.

Park at the trailhead sign and/or pit toilet (provided the fire has left either standing). The trail to your left will lead to the campsites, several smooth-rock fishing points, and eventually back up to Forest Road #2401, where you must follow the road for more than a half mile before the trail branches to the right and finishes its loop around Elk Lake's northern shore.

The trail leading the other way, straight down to the egress point of the lake, may turn out to be a dead end. A giant single log footbridge used to span the powerful rapids here. However, the footbridge became old and dangerous, so it was decommissioned without a new bridge to replace it.

In winter and spring, you will stand here and admire the roaring, fast rapids. But you don't dare ford them.

In summer and early autumn, when Elk Lake dries to a grassy field, you will face a bone dry gulley. Climb down and across, then pick up the loop trail on the other side. Another small grove of old growth cedars await you just past this point--again, provided the Maple Fire has spared them.

26/The Balds & Elk Lake Spur Trail

DIRECTIONS

Contained in the paragraphs following the heading "Fire Hazards." The Elk Lake connector trail is 1.6 miles up FR #2421.

SEASONAL CONCERNS	ROAD CONDITIONS	TRAIL DIFFICULTY	SAFETY CONCERNS	TRAILHEAD PASS?
SNOW LEVEL	ROUGH ROAD	EASY	CLIFFS KID CAUTION	NONE

Definitions of Terms: Pages 14-15

If you're in your 4WD vehicle, tooling around the national forest, sooner or later you come to a road that branches off the road you're on.

It's usually a smaller, choppier, less trusty-looking road. It seems tempting. But is it going to be dangerous, you ask.

Do you go?

You want to go.

Looks pretty scary. If only you already knew where the road goes . . .

Forest Road #2421 is one of those roads. I'll give you three good reasons for taking it: (1) the Strawberry Bald viewpoint; (2) some decent dispersed campsites; (3) the nearly unknown Elk Lake connector trail.

FR #2421 goes far beyond the three points of interest I am sharing with you, winding far up the Jefferson Ridge and crossing the Jefferson Ridge Trail at least twice. However, it is a rocky, dicey, barely maintained road that is one of the most hazardous I have ever been on.

Eventually, even the best vehicle with the best tires, and even the bravest driver, will hit a point of no return. I try to avoid those myself. It's a sweaty, scary business. Backing up on a logging road with a 500-foot cliff waiting to swallow you, hearing your tires crunching loose rock, feeling the pitch as your passenger side slides off the shoulder . . . no, sir, I'll pass on that.

FIRE HAZARDS

If any road has changed because of the Maple Fire, this would be the one.

Find it by taking the Hamma Hamma Road to the "Y" after 6.4 miles. SET ODOMETER. Turn left and cross the bridge. Barely a fifth of a mile later, FR #2421 branches upward on your right. Take it, provided it is not gated or otherwise blocked.

At .8 miles a very large boulder sits in the middle of the road (prior to the fire). You used to be able to get around it, on the right.

MOSSY BALDS

At 1.2 miles you'll come to a pullout on the left. Note the steep, rocky, open glades above and below you. A forest service employee once told me they were called "balds," and that the entire area is known as the Hamma Hamma Balds, named for the open, bald outcroppings on most of the slopes.

This spot is worth exploring. Follow the faint, short trail on your left down to the lower glade and, if you can remove your shoes, feel what it's like to walk (or sit or lie) on the spongy grasses, lichens and moss that cover these huge rock surfaces.

Time your visit right and eat wild strawberries all along the trail and road--thus its name, Strawberry Bald.

You're on a big, big ledge with lots of soft padding. You'll want to lie and roll around, despite the dizzying height. The southeast view is not spectacular; another ridge obstructs your view of Hood Canal, nor do you see any towering peaks.

However, you get a nice perspective when you note that you are directly across from Forest Road #2401, separated by distantly roaring Jefferson Creek cutting through its canyon 500 feet straight below.

Giant log in center of photo is a remaining portion of the last footbridge to cross Jefferson Creek below Elk Lake. The forest service has no immediate plans to put in a new bridge.

TWILIGHT FOR TWO

If you are romantically inclined, consider a blanket, some wine, and staying past twilight to watch the stars come out. No need to build a fire. During clear days in the summer, the rocks and moss are warmed by the sun, holding their heat into the evening.

Climb the bald above for an even more expansive view.

Continuing on, for the next third of a mile, you'll see a series of turnoffs and pullouts indicating places to camp. Not all these are ideal, however, and the Maple Fire may have torched the area considerably.

However, at 1.6 miles, the road hooks to the right after passing through a much larger clearing used historically for camping--a very fine location in comparison to the others.

This is also where to look for the small wooden sign on the left marking Elk Lake Trail, #805.

Starting at 1,100 feet in elevation, the trail remains level, smooth, and well maintained as it hugs the ridge opposite the Jefferson Creek Valley from Forest Road #2401. At 1.2 miles in length, it offers a few peek-a-boo glimpses down into the whitewater canyon, nearly 600 feet below.

In a very short time you reach the junction with the Elk Lake loop trail, and depending on the time of year and if the rapids are dry, you may cross the gully near the official trailhead, or, if the rapids are running, you will need to follow the loop to your right.

Prior to the fire, a summer round trip starting from the connector trailhead, and circling Elk Lake counterclockwise, would be about 4.5 miles and full of scenery, vistas, old growth and beautiful, hidden campsites.

It is very likely the Maple Fire began in one of these.

Left: The "beach" at the campsite on Upper Elk Lake. Right: Low-sunk picnic table and rock fire ring are the only amenities at the only campsite on the lake.

27/Upper Elk Lake

DIRECTIONS

From Highway 101, take the Hamma Hamma Road (FS #25) to the "Y" at 6.4 miles. SET ODOMETER. Go left on Forest Road #2480 for 3 miles, then right on Forest Road #2401, which climbs immediately. Passing the Elk Lake Trailhead at 2.5 miles (5.5 odometer miles), go about a mile until you come to another "Y" in the road, where you will bear left onto Forest Road #2441. In less than a quarter-mile you will see Upper Elk Lake on your left. The road climbs slightly with the campsite parking area also on the left.

SEASONAL CONCERNS	ROAD CONDITIONS	TRAIL DIFFICULTY	SAFETY CONCERNS	TRAILHEAD PASS?
SNOW LEVEL	4WD	EASY	PICNIC SAFE	NONE

*Definitions of Terms: Pages 14-15

Though not the paradise it once was, Upper Elk Lake, 1,200 feet high, remains a secluded and very special mountain lake hideaway.

Its water is spring-fed and clear. In April of years past, hundreds of reddish-orange newts would swim and swirl in the shallows near shore, mating merrily.

Upper Elk is about 10 acres, round, and fairly deep in the middle. It has always remained a bit of a secret because it is located on a minor logging road, and, in days past, was barely visible from the road.

That is not the case anymore. Beavers have had an enormous impact on this lake, clearing down most of its foliage bordering the road, and changing the water level with their dams.

THE GOOD

One amazing thing remains certain about Upper Elk Lake, however: come June, July and August, it heats up to very warm and swimmable temperatures, and, in a best-case scenario, would allow a fire at night near shore while bathers could be out on the lake, swimming under the moon or stars.

Not many other Olympic Mountain lakes can make that claim.

THE BAD, THE UGLY

Currently, there is only one viable camping spot on the lake, a flat, private nook tucked below the road and nestled among thick, secluding huckleberry bushes.

A park-issued picnic table was brought here long ago, then anchored deep in the dirt. A big, rock circle fire pit always welcomes you here. A cozy camp for two or four, there is room for one tent, comfortably, or two small tents placed close together.

I prefer to camp here in late spring. The water temperature might not be "swim perfection" yet, but the insects are not as numerous as they can be in summer. Also, this spot seems to take a beating, so to speak, from the summer weekends when it is always full of campers, who, over the years, have fallen nearby trees for firewood, as well as exhausted most options for burial of waste.

A short, mostly unknown trail leads from Forest Road #2401 to the opposite side of the lake, but there is no camp-worthy site here, then the trail suddenly ends. It's a gnarly, reedy, muddy swimming spot, full of roots and sharp, sunken branches.

It would be nice if other campsites could be developed around the lake perimeter. It might take some pressure off the one and only--and far too popular--spot I've been recommending.

If you can secure it on a warm summer weekday, and it's been left in good condition by its prior users, then, believe me, a moonlit night here (with skinny dipping, of course) might rank as a forever four-star memory.

28/Upper Washington Creek Swimming Hole

DIRECTIONS

On Highway 101, go north 6 miles past Lilliwaup to Jorsted Creek Road (Forest Road #24). SET ODOMETER HERE. Stay on FR #24, bearing left under the power lines at 2.2 miles, continuing to the white post with an "X" carved at the top at 4.6 miles. From here, it is .8 miles to FR #2441 (5.4 odometer miles), which bears steeply to your right. Crest Washington Pass and continue, heading downhill until you see a short turnoff marked by a single "200" road marker on your left at 8 miles on your odometer. This is the trailhead.

SEASONAL CONCERNS	ROAD CONDITIONS	TRAIL DIFFICULTY	SAFETY CONCERNS	TRAILHEAD PASS?
SNOW LEVEL	4WD ROUGH ROAD	MODERATE/ CANYON	WATER CROSSINGS	NONE

Definitions of Terms: Pages 14-15

If you're up for a wild and crazy adventure, this one ranks very near the top.

Upper Washington Creek has it all. You'll start on a mountain road, climb 1,800 feet to breathtaking Washington Pass, then continue further into the Olympics, parking to hike on an old, overgrown logging road that crosses a 200-foot landslide, to finally boulder your way down a bubbling creek to a pair of high mountain swimming holes joined by a classic "otterfall" cataract.

You will not see another human being. This truly is the path not taken. Best of all, despite its high adventure rating, it is a safe outing that is fine for kids.

Leaving the cool shadows of the lower pool, this visitor climbs above the otterfalls, returning to her blanket in the sun at Upper Washington Creek Swimming Hole.

This trip is ideal for hot and sunny days. The upper swimming hole bakes under direct sunlight, inspiring a "clothing optional" state of mind. This also makes for a perfect day hike picnic.

However, late in the summer, it's likely that the creek level drops too much to make this a worthy dip--so try taking this trip June through July.

DIRECTIONS TO HEAVEN

Refer to the earlier chapter on Washington Pass for additional directions and descriptions.

If you've never been to the pass, plan on parking and enjoying the view. On clear days you can see the big vanilla cone that is Mt. Rainier, as well as the tapering puzzle piece that is Tahuya Point jutting into Hood Canal.

Forest Road #2441 is an amazing shortcut that takes you to Elk Lake, Jefferson Lake, and eventually down to Lena Lake and the Hamma Hamma River. It is curvy, wild and marked by sheer drops down rocky canyons. I would not take this road in anything but a four-wheel-drive vehicle.

At eight miles on your odometer, you'll be going steeply downhill through an area marked by cliffs that slough off loose rock. Rocks as big as beach balls break loose and pile up beside the road.

Right here, look for the overgrown road jutting sharply left marked by a small sign indicating the number 200.

Find a level spot to park. Bring water, food, and your two canyoneering essentials: a walking stick and rubber-soled shoes or sandals.

HIKING IN

We'll be hiking FR #2441-200 all the way to Washington Creek. It's an old decommissioned logging road, and quite soon the road bed grows crowded with young alder and fir. It's a real tight, rogue mini-forest, so keep your eyes on the trail, as hundreds of ankle-high branches want to snare your feet.

Be patient. Follow the faint trail and keep pushing through. Eventually the road opens up again and the hiking grows easier.

However, a half-mile in, some serious landslides make for the only dangerous footing on the trail. From the top of the slide you can view your goal: the Upper Washington Creek Swimming Hole, 200 feet below. There, at the bottom of a brown, dusty chute of a landslide, lies a shimmering jade dollop of water with the white tail of an otterslide leading to a lower, shadier pool.

This is not a deep, expansive pool, but rather a gentle, sunny wading spot with enough cold, wet action to cool off hot bodies.

FINAL APPROACH

To get down to it, keep hiking while keeping a watch for a small rock cairn. The idea is to find a decent place to drop into the Washington Creek drainage, then work your way downstream until you reach the pools. The further up you keep hiking, the longer you must work back downstream.

The cairn indicates a fairly easy scramble down, maybe 50 feet from road to water. The creek is a gentle journey, made easier if you let your feet get wet. Allow a half hour to fully enjoy this wild riparian world, full of meandering, shady pools and fun, rock-hopping obstacles as you slip-slide your way down to the Upper Washington Swimming Hole.

By the way, you can keep going downstream. Washington Creek is the Number One canyoneering experience in this part of the Olympics. Eventually, you will reach the bridge and campsite at Forest Road #2401, near Elk Lake--but that might require a night's bivouac to achieve, as well as a couple of sections where you will face chest-high or deeper water.

THE SWIMMING HOLE

The rocks are bright white and the sunshine intense. The water is so clear that a single water spider gliding on the surface can throw individual shadows for the water bubbles on its feet. I kid you not.

Now, neither pool is more than four-feet deep, but each is alive with wet, teasing pleasure as you contemplate the moment you dare drop in. Let hot sun help you decide. Thick, yoga-mat moss covers the ledges on one side, making a perfect place to spread out a towel, lie back and soak up the rays.

Get good and hot, then get good and ready. Your water is waiting to greet you with a cold, strong embrace.

29/Washington Creek Canyon

DIRECTIONS

Hamma Hamma Road (FR #25) to the "Y" at 6.4 miles; go left. SET ODOMETER crossing the bridge. Stay on FR #2480 for 2.3 miles to the intersection with FR #2401, where you turn right, uphill, following signs for Elk Lake. Stay straight on FR #2401 where FR #2441 branches to the left. In about two-tenths of a mile after the branch, you will come to the bridge crossing Washington Creek. Campsite, swimming holes and canyon access to the left.

SEASONAL CONCERNS	ROAD CONDITIONS	TRAIL DIFFICULTY	SAFETY CONCERNS	TRAILHEAD PASS?
SNOW LEVEL	4WD	CANYON	SWIFT/DEEP WATER	NONE

*Definitions of Terms: Pages 14-15

One of the best features of the Washington Creek Canyon is the campsite at the entry point. It's a cushy flat spot perched on a bluff directly across the bridge where Washington Creek meets Forest Road #2401.

The site has seen a lot of wear and tear over the years, both manmade and naturally occurring, but still holds up as one of the best off-road spots to pitch a tent and huddle by a fire through the night.

Flood erosion has eaten away at the bank below the campsite, but recently the same forces have pushed a fresh pile of river rock in front of the bank, somewhat stabilizing the site.

This re-routing has also created a jade hued swimming hole about six feet deep––adding considerably to the campsite's real estate value. Less than 300 feet upstream from the campsite is another swimming hole on the left where the creek eddies in slow circles, forming a natural cul-de-sac. In summer the water is considerably warmer here than in the free-flowing stream, inspiring me to name it the "Little Woodstock" of Washington Creek.

UP THE CREEK

Beyond this second swimming hole, Washington Creek becomes one of the most challenging and fascinating canyoneering adventures in the southeastern Olympics.

The later in summer and the lower the water, the better. Use a walking stick and prepare to get wet. Waterproof gear bags highly recommended.

At first your journey consists of dry walking tons and tons of river rock, but quite soon you'll notice ledges on both sides growing into considerable cliffs. Shadows grow deep; small caves and niches sculpt the rocks on both sides.

The gorge runs deeper now. Water depth rises from mid-calf to over your knees. The canyon is a cobblestone road under water, an uneven course of flat and round rocks, and you'll need to plant your stick firmly as you plan each step ahead.

You will hit the first "pinch" in about a half mile, a place where the gorge runs very deep and you must either wade ahead, chest-deep, with your gear waterproofed somehow, or else scale the cliffs on one side and bushwhack forward.

The canyon changes personality every few hundred yards, with many small waterfalls and sections of tumbled boulders, followed by places where you must cross the gorge on a fallen log. Washington Creek Canyon runs three miles in this manner, every inch another delicious moment of "decision time."

You'll find this a wild, pristine, prehistoric journey, an unbelievable maze of gorgeous scenery and astounding obstacles. I have not made it completely from one end to the other, but have come far from points both above and below.

Eventually, you will reach the Upper Washington Creek Swimming Hole (previous chapter), from which you can exit the gorge and reach a parked car on Forest Road #2441.

However, this full trip may require an overnight stay. Plan and pack accordingly.

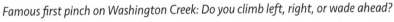

Famous first pinch on Washington Creek: Do you climb left, right, or wade ahead?

30/Lower Jefferson Falls

DIRECTIONS

Hamma Hamma Road (FS #25) to the "Y" at 6.4 miles; go left. Stay on FR #2480 for about 3 miles to the intersection with FR #2401, where you turn right, uphill, following signs for Elk Lake. Stay straight on FR #2401 where FR #2441 branches to the left. After bearing right at the branch, you will come to the first bridge crossing Washington Creek. Within .3 miles you will come to the second bridge and Lower Jefferson Falls.

SEASONAL CONCERNS	ROAD CONDITIONS	TRAIL DIFFICULTY	SAFETY CONCERNS	TRAILHEAD PASS?
SNOW LEVEL	4WD	EASY	CLIFFS	NONE

Definitions of Terms: Pages 14-15

Life will still go on if you never visit Lower Jefferson Falls. In fact, many people drive right past it and never know it's there. It's not particularly big, or lovely, or provide a cool place to play.

It is, however, viewed from a cliff edge and also from a high bridge above. For the price of a quick stop and park, it is worth it.

You'll find it on the forest road to Jefferson Lake, where you cross two similar concrete bridges in succession. These cross the two main creeks that feed Elk Lake, Washington Creek, then Jefferson Creek.

Lower Jefferson Falls are located below the second bridge, which spans Jefferson Creek.

Park before or immediately after the bridge, keeping a watchful eye for wild strawberries and red huckleberries if you visit in season.

You'll hear the falls. Find your best views by hopping the guardrail to approach the high bluff overlooking Lower Jefferson Falls. They spill about 16 feet into a deep, frothy pool. There is no safe access to this pool where the water churns and drops two more times below the bridge.

From above you can inch closer on the cliffs to get a view of the water pulsing and churning below the bridge, a waterway made more dangerous by being partially choked with trees and driftwood.

The cliffs here are fun but scary. I've had sandwiches and tea here, but at the same time, I highly recommend you hold onto any small child's hand.

By the way, you are in the middle of some of the best car camping in this part of the national forest. Great spots are located near both bridges.

On the opposite side of the bridge there is a large campsite with a trail that leads down to a lovely but frigid swimming hole. From here you also have a nice view back toward the lower falls and bridge.

Right: Lower Jefferson Falls drops in three stages, the third spilling into a deep, cold pool below the bridge. Below: Snowy upper falls thunder into an unapproachable, turgid bowl visible from cliffs and bridge above.

31/Boulder Field & Jefferson Lake

DIRECTIONS

Hamma Hamma Road (FR #25) to the "Y" at 6.4 miles; go left. Stay on FR #2480 for 2.3 miles to the intersection with FR #2401, then climb right on FR #2401, traveling about 9 miles until the scenic pullout where you pass through the middle of the rockslide, indicating the parking spot, on your left, for Boulder Field. Alternatively, travel less than another half-mile to the regular trailhead to Jefferson Lake.

SEASONAL CONCERNS	ROAD CONDITIONS	TRAIL DIFFICULTY	SAFETY CONCERNS	TRAILHEAD PASS?
SNOW LEVEL	4WD	MODERATE BUSHWHACK	MILD KID CAUTION	NONE

*Definitions of Terms: Pages 14-15

Jefferson Lake was formed many centuries ago, when an ancient earthquake triggered a massive rockslide, sending tons of boulders rolling into Jefferson Creek. The creek plugged and expanded into an elongated "O" between two hillsides high up in the watershed.

Connected by the same road as Elk Lake, Jefferson Lake is larger, deeper and more substantial than Elk Lake; while it also shrinks in the waning days of summer, it does not disappear as does Elk Lake.

In winter the road stays deep under snow. But come spring and summer, Forest Road #2401 becomes navigable again, allowing campers, hikers and explorers to visit Jefferson Lake and points beyond.

OVERGROWN SHORES

There is a briefly visible national forest trailhead kiosk and sign at the trailhead for Jefferson Lake. Coupled with the large, wide parking area and similarly brief views of lake water to your left, you should be able to find your way to the lake shore with no problem.

The trail snakes down a steep, short slope, winding past old growth cedars and firs, as many on the ground as still remain standing.

I do not know why, but the forest here is taking a beating in terms of fallen, old growth trees.

Now, I may have lost the official trail or tried to push through on the wrong amateur trails, but I've had problems in recent years reaching the actual lake shore. I've found openings in the understory and taken some nice photographs of the lake's eerie, greenish hued water, but the shore was either too muddy to walk on or too protected behind thick thorns and brush to even approach.

In fact, let me pass on that there is a smaller, even more overgrown, Upper Jefferson Lake, if you can find your way to work yourself further up the creek.

BE BOULDER INSTEAD

So, it was my frustration with the gnarly, overgrown shore, plus the lack of really good photos when you get down there--deep shadow on the opposite side, no mountains--that inspired another approach.

About a half-mile before the trailhead to Jefferson Lake, you come up through the Boulder Field, the rocky remnants of the ancient landslide that plugged up the lake.

You can't miss the huge, gleaming boulders on your right, stacked high all the way up the mountain shoulder.

At one point the road opens to a mountain view ahead, just as you pass between several big boulders, with a stack of them forming a nice climbing point that tapers maybe 80 to 100 feet high on your left--a great little rocky scramble.

Immediately past it, you'll see a nice camping and parking spot also on the left, marked by a stone fire pit.

If you come to a pair of wide open, overused parking spots on your right, then you've gone too far.

Go back and park at the spot with the fire ring.

Now, this entire area is built for bouldering. You can climb to your heart's content, and turn the kids loose for hours on their own. Rocks take a lot of weathering up here and are wrapped in a very durable layer of moss. When dry, their footing is very good.

LAKE AND BAKE

From here you can also explore a more exciting and challenging way down to Jefferson Lake. In fact, in about 15 minutes or less, you can be approaching the far corner of the lake where the ancient landslide plugged up the creek. From there you can see Mt. Washington and two other peaks, enjoying the very best views of the lake.

Come early for sunrise shots, and stay until the sun rolls over the tree tops and bakes the big rocks at this secluded location. There are plenty of places to spread a towel for sunbathing, swimming and picnic delights.

THE WAY

Climb that high point next to the road I mentioned earlier, about a one-minute scramble. It's the highest stack of rocks around, beginning right at the road and topping out no more than 200 feet from it.

From the top you can hear Jefferson Creek--a very important orienteering marker. That's the sound you want to head towards, but keeping it on your left.

Also from here, looking west, you'll see a big, stand-alone boulder, bigger than a house. This is a rock climber's destination and has a name I can't currently recall. Climbers who use the parking spot have worn a short trail to it, and whether you start from the parking spot or from the rocky hilltop point, you'll want to get to the base of this boulder to start you final approach to the lakeshore.

Head downslope, keeping the giant boulder to your right, then behind you. Listen for the creek, far off to your left. You are now in the middle of Boulder Field where you will need to hop a lot of rocks. This is fun but keep a cautious, careful pace.

Let the downhill slope draw you to the lake, following faint trails where others have gone. Avoid gullies, however. They are gnarly and congested with branches.

In fact, with little soil to decompose woody debris, the entire rocky forest floor is littered with bone-like branches that have been stacking up for years--a great place to gather new walking sticks.

A last barrier of salmon berry and thick brush guard the lake's edge. Into late spring, dried grasses still press down from winter snow. Driftwood, mud, slick rocks, loose stone and gnarly brush--all these entanglements require careful attention as you move along the shore.

A huge driftwood gyre bobs at this end of the lake. If you make walking canes for a living, you can retire after a visit here. You can even see bubbles where the lake water is drawn underground, to reappear as Jefferson Creek many yards below.

The view is totally worth it. Marshmallow snow on Mt. Washington-- in total, three beautiful peaks primping in Lake Jefferson's mirrored surface.

Left: Mt. Washington peers over scattered driftwood towads east edge of Jefferson Lake, where water swirls as it pulls down and through the ancient landslide damming this end. Below: Rocky view from Boulder Field, where you park your car to begin short bushwhack to Jefferson Lake egress point.

32/Upper Jefferson Falls

DIRECTIONS

Hamma Hamma Road (FR #25) to the "Y" at 6.4 miles; go left. Stay on FR #2480 for 2.3 miles to the intersection with FR #2401, where you turn right, uphill, driving 9 miles to Jefferson Lake. Continue a few miles more to the bridge where you will see Upper Jefferson Falls high up on your right.

SEASONAL CONCERNS	ROAD CONDITIONS	TRAIL DIFFICULTY	SAFETY CONCERNS	TRAILHEAD PASS?
SNOW LEVEL	4WD POTHOLES	SHORT & MODERATE	PICNIC WITH CAUTION	NONE

Definitions of Terms: Pages 14-15

This waterfall is a sweet, sweet joy, mainly in that, as an experience and an attraction, this is the waterfall "gift" that keeps on giving.

First of all, it's a jaw-dropping, spectacular drive just to find the falls, especially if you time your trip to the spring season.

Then, you catch your first glimpse of the falls from the logging road, but not entirely. There's more and you can sense it. Your appetite for adventure awakens. You're intrigued, seeing them like a white, flowing fabric unfurled high upon the hill.

Meanwhile, you realize that you have just found a supreme car camping site right where you are, parked beside a bridge at the foot of the falls.

It gets better . . . but I mustn't forget to tell this story in the proper order.

OVERVIEW

Upper Jefferson Falls practically drops out of nowhere to come roaring off a valley floor, down into a ragged gorge, then magically beside the most pristine and alluring "lovers' ledge," then drops another 200 feet in a series of thundering cataracts before spilling into a final pool beside the campsite at the road.

Then it tumbles another 150 feet or so before it levels out to feed Upper Jefferson Lake, but we don't even count this part because this section occurs after the creek has passed under the road and shot out of a manmade culvert.

The beauty and poetry of the falls and its surroundings are of the level of Sol Duc Falls and other famously idyllic Olympic waterfalls. This is a real gem--one of the best--and I will catch hell for publicizing it; however, I honestly believe that, should 100 or 200 more people come to visit these falls because of this book, yes, there will be some damage to the hillside and loss of moss, but I also I feel that there will be several among those 200 who will have a bonafide nature/religious experience, and quite possibly never be the same again.

That is the spirit of exploring, and the reason I share what I know: I want you to blow your mind; I want you bedazzled by God's creation.

THE ROAD THERE

Don't even try this trip until spring is underway, perhaps mid- or late April, as the road is totally impassable during winter snows.

Pick up your directions from the previous chapters on Boulder Field and Jefferson Lake, continuing past Jefferson Lake, up the same road for another 4 to 5 miles, I am estimating. (I lost my odometer readings for these destinations, sorry.)

This road gets a little bumpy and channel cut with watery rivulets, but hang in there unless you encounter a blocking landslide or deep pocket of snow. Your payoff will be nearly a dozen runoff streams pouring off the steep hillsides on your right. These are your very own private waterfalls, gifts of the gods. Your climax will be a section of cliff face maybe 30 feet high and 40 feet across where the snowmelt is pouring down like a wide liquid curtain. This waterfall is almost part of the road. You can literally park and touch the falls, then go on your merry way.

This is a major landmark. Later in the spring and summer, the cliff face goes dry.

The next landmark is the concrete bridge that crosses Jefferson Creek. Park on the right immediately past the bridge, unless someone is already there. This is the primo campsite I mentioned earlier. Your eyes will grow wide staring at the wading pool shaped like a Coors commercial; this is the all-time iconic mountain stream and it is all yours if you can land this campsite.

In late spring wild blueberries and plump red huckleberries crowd the hillsides with their full, heavy fruit. There is enough here for buckets, purple fingers and minds dreaming of pies. Huge ripe salmon berries grow among the falls, the fruit bobbing in the spilling water, the sun shining like mad on the berries and silvery stream.

So, what about the falls?

CLIMBING

Pick up a faint, winding animal trail on the left side of the falls, and climb upwards for several hundred feet. At times the falls will be only inches or a few tree roots from your feet. Amazingly, you will always find the next foothold or handhold to go up and up, heading toward the large fantail section of the falls--the highest part you were able to see from the road.

There's a spot here where you must go underneath a large log and then come out, round it and climb a ledge. This place is loaded with blueberries. Soon as you top the ledge, you will recognize that you've left

one world behind you and a whole new other one is greeting you like a door opening on paradise.

This is the Lovers' Ledge, a wide, calm level spot alongside a deep and fast-moving water chute that spills out into the fantail falls just below. An old fire ring suggests a long-ago night of earthly pleasures.

Everywhere you look is dappled in moss: huge, prehistoric cliffs on both sides, the trees, the ledge itself. And there, above you, another fierce section of waterfalls, a rocky scar cut deep in the cliff, maybe 80 feet high or more, pumping a turbulent plunge of white, roaring water.

That's what I meant about the falls that keeps on giving; this new ledge and upper falls are nothing like the climb you made to get here, nor is it like the falls and pools down near the bridge, which seem so far away and long ago.

Upper Jefferson Falls are interactive, dynamic and ever-changing. You don't view them. You experience them.

Lovers' Ledge is the place to wait out the end of the world.

Better yet, it's a great place to begin a new one.

Left: Upper Jefferson Falls, so far. A scant animal trail traces the falls on their left, leading to a broad, mossy ledge and yet another section of falling water. Below: Bridge and single campsite at bottom of falls.

33/Little Yosemite Valley (Jefferson Creek Watershed Source)

DIRECTIONS

Refer to previous chapter. The Little Yosemite Valley is less than a mile beyond Upper Jefferson Falls.

SEASONAL CONCERNS	ROAD CONDITIONS	TRAIL DIFFICULTY	SAFETY CONCERNS	TRAILHEAD PASS?
SNOW LEVEL	4WD ROUGH ROAD	EASY	SAFE	NONE

Definitions of Terms: Pages 14-15

If Upper Jefferson Falls (previous chapter) hasn't sufficiently blown your mind, get ready for this one.

We are going to drive about a half mile past the bridge at the base of the falls, rounding and climbing and passing an old, decommissioned logging road that branches to our left. Stay on FR #2401 and you'll come to a final, steep curve nestled deep in the forested, shadowy slope.

I mention this shadow because here you will find the deepest, longest-lasting snow field on any major logging road in this part of the Olympics. Long after all the other roads are clear, including the upper trailhead to Mt. Ellinor, this infamous patch will be waiting for you. And unless you have enormous traction tires with a heavy, high-clearance vehicle, this is the end of the road for you.

I cannot accurately predict when this snow field melts, sometime in May, usually, but please know that just beyond it, the road straightens out, goes back into sunlight, and delivers you to the Number One Mountain View in all of Mason County.

If snow stops you, walk through it to see this spot: a breathtaking look deep behind Mt. Washington, to Pershing and Jefferson Peak, a horseshoe of 6,000-foot snowy peaks forming a scale likeness of Yosemite Valley with all its rocky glory.

And in spring, when the snow melts off in silver braids, you can count maybe a dozen waterfalls trailing their filaments over cliffs and ledges more than 2,000 feet high.

I have brought or sent dozens of people here and they all agree that this is a profoundly beautiful valley, a living post card of what mountain scenery is supposed to be.

Imagine this as your short day-hike from your camp at the bottom of Upper Jefferson Falls. It is like going to heaven, *then* winning the lottery.

Be aware, however, that it is a gnarly, claustrophobic bushwhack if you choose to explore, on foot, higher up the valley.

If the road is clear, continue on, passing over the culvert shielding Jefferson Creek. You are in the heart of the valley now. High meadow flowers and big bumble bees. Fifty shades of green.

Next, the road begins to climb steeply for nearly another mile until it becomes impassable--perhaps a judgment call--at over 3,000 feet. A half mile further is the cutoff and parking area for Goober Pond, a classic old timer's fishing hole.

Study the road and proceed cautiously, if at all. It might be smarter to park and continue on foot if you want to get higher.

One of the best mountain views in Mason County is "Little Yosemite," below, the valley just past Upper Jefferson Falls.

From Top: Looking across
Lake Cushman from the top
of Mt. Ellinor; Looking same
direction over Lake Cushman,
in distance, from much lower
Dow Mountain; lower section
of Copper Creek, found off trail.

North Fork of the Skokomish River

34. Mt. Ellinor 90

35. Big Creek Falls - Jefferson Pass
   to Mt. Washington 92

36. Big Creek Confluence & Trail 96

37. Dow Mountain 98

38. Cushman Falls - Mt. Rose Trailhead 100

39. Lake Cushman Swim Spots. 102

40. Shady Lane Trail to Staircase Loop 104

41. Copper Creek Mines & Trail 107

42. Alley Falls - Snow Lake Falls. 109

34/Mt. Ellinor

DIRECTIONS

From Hoodsport, take Highway 119 for 9.2 miles until it ends in a "T". Go right for 1.5 miles until you see Forest Road #2419, on your left, which climbs steadily toward Mt. Ellinor's lower and upper trailheads, at approximately 6 and 7 miles. Be sure to turn left on FR #2419-014 to reach the upper trailhead.

SEASONAL CONCERNS	ROAD CONDITIONS	TRAIL DIFFICULTY	SAFETY CONCERNS	TRAILHEAD PASS?
SNOW LEVEL	4WD POTHOLES	DIFFICULT	HAVE GOOD GEAR	UPPER T.H.: FOREST PASS

Definitions of Terms: Pages 14-15

Mt. Ellinor is the signature peak with the most sought-after view in Mason County. Indeed, it is a favorite of hikers and climbers throughout Thurston, Pierce and King counties, popular for its easy access, steep but very attainable climb, and its wild "snow chute" return route for those who prefer to fly, rather than walk, for their descent.

Until last year it was also famous for its mountain goats. These creatures, long despised by the National Park Service, are being forcefully evicted from the Olympics, due to their illegal alien status, i.e., non-native to this ecosystem. The process may take another year or two, but eventually all of them will be gone--either transported or shot.

TWO TRAILHEADS

You can add another several more miles to your Mt. Ellinor climb by starting off at the Big Creek Trailhead, which connects far below after starting at 600 feet in elevation.

Most folks prefer the standard lower and upper trailheads, however. Usually you drive to these. The lower provides a beautiful, slow ascent through some of the finest old growth timber, and adds about 1.5 miles and maybe 1,000 feet to your climb. It gets more visitor traffic as the spring begins, when the road to the upper trailhead is still under snow.

As the summer commences, the upper trailhead gains wildly in popularity. Thirty years ago, when I first climbed Ellinor, you'd get a dozen cars on a busy day at the upper trailhead.

Today, I've counted over 70 cars at the upper and an equal number at the lower trailheads on a regular weekday in summer. Cars, people and especially dogs populate both trailheads like never before.

THE CLIMB

From the upper trailhead, Ellinor is a steady, challenging climb, but full of change and diversity, like a puzzle you become very involved in solving. There are cozy, level resting spots where water pools under shadows, then sections where you must tighten your pack straps, and climb stacked rock while searching for handholds.

Felt most famously is the thrill Ellinor gives you when you break above the tree line and look up at her snowfield, a long, white slant with nothing but footprints and distant climbers to show you the way.

On a hot, sunny day this is heaven. Already your view is priceless, and you can have it any moment you want, simply by turning around. Yet, onward and upward you go, sidestepping one trudge after the other.

The thought of sliding down that same mass of snow--it's quite the motivator, knowing you get a wild, reckless roller coaster as a reward for bagging this peak.

After the snowfield, you cross the saddle, another sweet, "I'm really doing this!" sensation as you ascend your way across to the south ledge and traditional "regrouping" spot before the final scramble, to the top, at 5,920 feet.

THE PEAK

Looking west from Ellinor's peak, you see into the craggy Olympics. The raised glacial bulk of Mt. Olympus is visible on clear days, as are many other peaks in the range. In contrast by looking east, you see Lake Cushman, Hood Canal, and the vast flatlands of Puget Sound.

Despite the crowds, Ellinor provides plenty of rocky viewpoints for groups to hang out and enjoy their stay. You can scramble from one point to another, or use the high spots for protective shade.

This is a worthy, memorable goal: conquering an Olympic peak in about two hours for most folks. Expect snow on top well into July, but at the end of most summers, Mt. Ellinor goes dry and dusty.

One downside: swarming black flies are a serious consideration; you are advised to prepare accordingly.

35/Big Creek Falls & Jefferson Pass to Mt. Washington

DIRECTIONS

From Hoodsport, take Highway 119 for 9.2 miles until it ends in a "T". Go right for 1.5 miles until you see Forest Road #2419, on your left, which climbs steadily toward Mt. Ellinor's lower and upper trailheads, at approximately 6 and 7 miles. Continue straight BEYOND the left turn onto FR #2419-014, going a few hundred feet until the road dead-ends.

SEASONAL CONCERNS	ROAD CONDITIONS	TRAIL DIFFICULTY	SAFETY CONCERNS	TRAILHEAD PASS?
SNOW LEVEL	4WD POTHOLES	PASS TRAIL DIFFICULT	PICNIC SAFE	NONE

Definitions of Terms: Pages 14-15

I should wear a T-shirt proclaiming "I Love to Rave," right?

So it will be no surprise that I rave and rave about Big Creek Falls. Like Upper Jefferson Falls, it's not simply a waterfall you stand and look at. Big Creek Falls is a magical location with lots of "super natural" things for visitors to do.

DESCRIPTION

Big Creek is a lacy, ponytail falls that shimmers in morning light on the east side of Mt. Ellinor, where Big Creek begins. Her last drop is 65 elegant feet into the sweetest swimming hole half-hidden behind a ledge. (Yes, she's warm enough for swimming, but we'll get to that later.)

If you step back along the old, crumbling logging road beside her, you will eventually see that Big Creek Falls has many more tiers of white, falling water. Far up the northeast side of Mt. Ellinor, she tumbles down from the snowfields. Measure her sections together and you could make a case for this waterfall being 300 feet or higher.

Regardless, her last drop is plenty beautiful for qualifying Big Creek as one of the top photogenic falls in this part of the Olympics. It's the way her spray kisses the rock face as it tumbles down, not quite a solid, sheer drop, but just enough friction to give her a pleasant curve, combined with thick bouncing braids, for a one-of-a-kind form.

She's also tucked back in a grotto. If you are not looking for her, you can pass her right by.

The falls are quite impressive--that is, until they go dry. Thanks to climate change, Big Creek Falls, a seasonal snowpack waterfall that usually runs steadily into August, now seems to shrink to a drizzle by June, definitely affecting her majestic appearance and ability to inspire.

Ideally, try to see her by late May.

OTHER FEATURES

(1) Wild strawberries up the wazoo, in season; (2) Located by walking along a decommissioned logging road that lies over 3,000 high with panoramic views of Hood Canal, Mt. Rainier, and everything east; (3) Near the most pristine natural drinking water source you can find; and (4) Very close to the Jefferson Pass Trailhead.

Let's consider (4) first. If you are tired of crowds at nearby upper Mt. Ellinor Trailhead, the Jefferson Pass Trail is waiting for you. This baby is a tight stitching of switchbacks and near-vertical footpaths that never waste a horizontal inch as you climb toward the rocky, exposed saddle between 5,920-foot Mt. Ellinor and Mt. Washington, at 6,255 feet.

The trail is narrow, underused and easy to lose, in places. It is a total joy, a true climber's route, as eventually it will break up and cease being a trail once you reach the final, rocky route to Mt. Washington's summit, recommended only for serious climbers fitted with gear.

We take the trail until we've climbed above tree line, getting the same east-facing views as Mt. Ellinor, but, again, without all the parking and crowd hassles. It's about 1.2 miles long and perhaps 1,500 feet in altitude gain, a fantastic, heart-pounding climb.

To find the trail, go another 400 yards further down the logging road from Big Creek Falls. Listen for running water. Just after the first tiny creek running off the hillside, you'll see a very small opening in the bushes on your left. No signs. The trail starts here, just BEFORE a second, larger creek.

MAKE IT WILD

Traveler's Tip: In the heat of summer, climb Jefferson Pass as high as you can, staying in the sun for photos and a light picnic lunch. Then descend at a safe but rapid pace, and head immediately back to Big Creek Falls. Try to keep a good sweat going.

Next, strip.

Go ahead, toss off those dirty, grimy clothes. Take a deep breath. Guide your tender feet over the cold, sharp stones--you can do this!--to stand in the back pool, knee-high deep, feeling the waterfall spray on your tingling skin. Take another breath. Drop slowly down until you sit in the water, feeling Nature's cold but affirmative embrace.

Splash. Wash. Call out weird phrases to each other. Hear your voice echo in this half-cave. Realize where you are: down to your shorts in a shallow grotto, bathing beneath a 65-foot Olympic Mountain waterfall with a 3,000-foot view almost to Canada rolling out below you.

About three minutes is all it takes. Come out. Sit down. Be ALIVE. Sun dry. Wear a big smile, then go put on something else.

Remember this forever.

HEAVY DRINKER

To find the falls, go straight instead of turning left onto Forest Road #2419-014 (route to upper Mt. Ellinor Trailhead). The road ends abruptly in front of a rockslide. Pack your gear, lock your car. You'll hear the falls before you see them, following the old logging road now buried under rock and soil. About 300 yards from your car, you'll see that you are now in front of a sheer cliff face towering over a thin strip of brush growing where the road meets the mountain.

Look for snowmelt in watery channels at the base of the cliff. Water will run alongside your feet. Listen for a tiny, tinkling spring. Push through the brush and you will find a gurgling, natural spigot where water trickles out of the cliff face in a tiny cleft made for the mouth of a water bottle. Here you can cup your hands and drink.

This snow-source water has just finished traveling through hundreds of feet of 35-million-year-old stone, picking up healthy minerals and filtering itself, as though passing through charcoal. If you can't bring yourself to drink from here, you need to . . . well, you need to re-examine your role in the cosmos, I suppose.

How much do you trust?

I and others have been drinking from here for years. I never miss a chance to fill my water bottles whenever I'm around.

Think of this as another one-of-a-kind Olympic Mountain memory: have a drink on me.

THE ROAD GOES ON

Besides providing wild strawberries in June, the old logging road goes for another mile or two, hugging the upper shoulder of Mt. Washington while providing 3,000-foot panoramic views.

There are more springs along the road and plenty of wide turnouts from the old logging days, which now make incredible, very private campsites for those who have wheels on their coolers and are willing to pull a wagon loaded with firewood.

THE RIGHT SPARK

Downed wood is pretty scarce along here, and you don't want to cut living trees for firewood. Also, do not start a fire up here in common-sense dry or burn-ban times; winds can whip up along these exposed mountain flanks and spread hot sparks for quite a distance.

One final consideration? Instead of the usual crowds and predictability of most fireworks shows, come up here to view Fourth of July rockets going off.

Why look up at fireworks when you can be looking down? It's like watching little toy towns far, far away, launching tiny colored explosions in clusters as far as you can see.

Every Independence Day evening, let Big Creek Falls host a memory that you will keep forever. Just be sure to leave your own fireworks at home-- never get that stupid, okay?

Upper Big Creek Falls

36/Big Creek Trail & Confluence

DIRECTIONS

From Hoodsport, take Highway 119 for 9.2 miles until it ends in a "T". From here you will see the entrance to Big Creek Campground nearly right in front of you. Jog quick left and park along the road, unless you have a Northwest Forest Pass or other qualifying pass allowing you to park at the official Big Creek Trailhead.

SEASONAL CONCERNS	ROAD CONDITIONS	TRAIL DIFFICULTY	SAFETY CONCERNS	TRAILHEAD PASS?
CREEK DIMINISH	DECENT ROAD	MODERATE	PICNIC SAFE	FOREST PASS

Definitions of Terms: Pages 14-15

Big Creek Trail has hundreds of loyal fans, due, in part, to its proximity to Hoodsport, Shelton and Union--after all, it is the first genuine national forest trail you come to when approaching the popular Lake Cushman and Staircase entrance to Olympic National Park.

It's also a delightful and basically easy trail, a 4.3 mile loop with a gradual, 1,000-foot elevation gain, an excellent workout for people of all ages and abilities. Though it has no scenic views and only a small grove of old growth trees in its lower basin, it is still a lovely and well-manicured trail, famous for its classic wooden footbridges that must be repaired and fortified every year.

It also has one of the largest patches of native wild blackberry, the tasty, "crawling vine" variety that are 500% better than the invasive Himalayan species. Find this treasure about a half-mile to one mile in, traveling counter clockwise from the bottom trailhead.

BRIDGES, RAPIDS

Overall, Big Creek Trail passes beneath tall, stately second growth timber, climbing steadily as it circles above a wooded valley where two streams come together, forming the Big Creek Confluence.

A new main bridge has been built near the covered cooking and picnic shelter; this used to wash out every few years until the forest service finally got serious and put in a real bridge, like at Staircase.

But there are also four or five hand-assembled footbridges throughout the length of the trail, and all of these are photographic as well as mechanical marvels. Pay special attention to the buttressing rock work and creek bed reinforcement. This difficult work is performed every year by the regionally famous Mount Rose Trail Crew. They are the gods of trail repair.

When you reach the apex of the trail, about two miles in from either side, you will see signs indicating the confluence. This is a short, connecting route to the place where the creeks run into each other.

I recommend you follow your explorer's instincts here, and meander off trail when you reach the tumbling waters. There are some great boulders to scramble on and around, and some fantastic "Northwest mountain stream" photos to be taken here. I have seen some spots that looked good for wading or quick swims, but the water seemed a bit fast, which also makes it colder since it doesn't have a chance to settle close to your skin-- still water, though cold, helps keep you warm. Moving water pulls the cold right through.

Still, there are plenty of big rocks to sit on and enjoy the sunshine, with maybe a foot soak or splash on the face enough of a cold dip here.

You'll also find some nice resting benches along this trail. And one small troll doll that hangs out around the Skinwood Creek footbridge.

The confluence area of Big Creek Falls features a classic Northwest series of photogenic cataracts.

37/Dow Mountain

DIRECTIONS

The main entrance to Price Lake and Dow Mountain is exactly 7.8 miles up State Route 119 from Hoodsport, on your right. (Just past the Skokomish Park "Group Camp" sign on your left.) Set your ODOMETER immediately upon turning onto Highway 119 from Hoodsport, so that you will coordinate with later odometer readings.

SEASONAL CONCERNS	ROAD CONDITIONS	TRAIL DIFFICULTY	SAFETY CONCERNS	TRAILHEAD PASS?
SNOW LEVEL	4WD ROUGH ROAD	EASY	SAFE	NONE

*Definitions of Terms: Pages 14-15

Please don't visit Dow Mountain expecting a pure, pristine, or perfect rainforest experience. No giant trees, jade pools or classic cataracts will greet you on the Dow.

But if you wish to study--and to some degree, appreciate--the environmental looks and effects of a "working" forest, the views from 2,514-foot-high Dow Mountain will demonstrate undisputedly what happens to working forests that must work overtime on behalf of the Washington State Department of Natural Resources (DNR).

Dow Mountain is an isolated, lower peak arising from the swampy basin in the shadows of Mt. Ellinor and Mt. Washington. A gnarly network of logging roads allow easy access to Dow Mountain's crown, which means you can drive straight up to about a dozen wide open parking or potential camping locations, the long-logged remains of what got left behind.

There are no toilets, benches, tables or any facilities at these spots, but you'll often find a stone fire ring, piles of slashed, dry firewood, and, of course, those sweeping views of Ellinor, Washington, Mt. Rose and the Brothers, as well as Price Lake, Melbourne Lake, Hood Canal, and the giant mass of Mt. Rainier towering above all flatlands east.

You'll also see generations of logging in evidence all across the distant hills and basin, a panoramic patchwork of differing-sized trees--everything from "four o'clock forest shadow" to "Paul Bunyan's Brazilian."

I go here to take photos and witness heavy weather. You can set up a pair of camp chairs, stay warm by a pre-dawn fire, and drink a thermos of hot coffee while you wait for the first pink blush of sunrise.

I've been on top of Dow Mountain during a rushing, roaring jet stream of white, puffy clouds, a long popcorn string of them, flowing down from Canada. We stood above the racing clouds as they took turns upstaging a conch-colored Mt. Rainier.

DRIVING DIRECTIONS

Though you might make it in summer without four-wheel drive, I recommend 4WD because of the sudden steep portions of the roads around Dow Mountain.

Less than a half mile from where you turned off Highway 119, you'll come to a triangular road island where a left turn takes you to Price Lake. A swamp will be on your left.

Go straight instead. The road soon comes to the first of two "Ys". Each time, bear to the left, lower option.

(From the first "Y" on, all roads basically lead to Dow Mountain. Come with a full tank, some patience, and allow yourself to drive all over the place. It's fun.)

Now, if you've stayed with the left-bearing directions, at 10.5 miles (from Hoodsport), you should cross a small wooden bridge spanning a summer-dry ravine.

At exactly 11 miles, the road splits off sharply to your right. Now, if you keep straight here you'll eventually come through Blue Gate #5 and wind up under the power lines above the Lilliwaup Gorge, where, even with low water in summer, you can hear rapids roar far down the canyon.

But at 11 miles, I recommend taking that sharp right, then following it upwards until you reach a logged clearing with a view of the mountains ringing Lake Cushman. Follow the dirt road as it swings left and circles this high northeastern shoulder of the mountain. You'll top out at a bald turnaround with a 2,000-foot view overlooking Hood Canal at Dewatto Bay.

This is a good place to take photos, have lunch, or make a cell call. From here, I recommend you just drive around, taking other routes back down the mountain. Be ready to find special places or, conversely, to be creeped out by the "target practice" appearance of some clearings.

True, there's a bit of blue collar camping around here; too many bottles, bullets and cans, but it's still a lovely, lonely and haunting place to witness extreme weather, or catch a sunrise or sunset without having to drive too far, pack too much, or put up with park rules, rangers, passes and crowds.

38/Cushman Falls & Mt. Rose Trailhead

DIRECTIONS

From Hoodsport, take Highway 119 for 9.2 curvy miles until it ends in a "T". Go left. At about 2.5 miles, slow down to be sure you see Cushman Falls. The Mt. Rose Trailhead and Recreation Area are just beyond that.

SEASONAL CONCERNS	ROAD CONDITIONS	TRAIL DIFFICULTY	SAFETY CONCERNS	TRAILHEAD PASS?
SNOWY TRAIL	POTHOLES	TRAIL DIFFICULT	PICNIC SAFE	NONE

Definitions of Terms: Pages 14-15

Cushman Falls pressure washes straight down in a vertical drop of 55 feet, delivering quite a splash where she smacks bottom. Even in the driest days of summer, she pours down with the solid, steady force of several fire hoses aimed at the same spot.

Despite her decent height, her force and fury, she is one of the most uninspiring waterfalls on the Olympic Peninsula. The main reason is because she is located right next to the forest road beside Lake Cushman. Perhaps 90 percent of the people who drive the road do not even notice her, that's how fast you blow past this under appreciated jewel.

She doesn't photograph well, either. Obscured by brush and recessed into a Plain Jane rock ledge, she comes out of nowhere with the presence of a shower stall, as though Cushman Falls was a last-minute manmade replica, built on a budget, too.

FUN STARTS HERE

However, within a few hundred feet of her long, white, liquid chute, you come to the area's first map and information kiosk, and basically, the gateway to the newly developed picnic and swimming area at the base of the Mt. Rose Trailhead, a very popular trail.

I wish I had an exact odometer reading for Cushman Falls, but I don't.

Giant old growth stump along Lake Cushman shore, just below Mt. Rose Trailhead.

Generally, after you turn left at the Highway 119 "T," you drive a mile or so until the road becomes famously UNPAVED. Then you drive another mile or so to the falls and recreation area for Mt. Rose, which is marked by the kiosk, restrooms, picnic tables, and well-built step trails with handrails leading down to the lake.

Go slow to not miss the falls, which come up suddenly on your right. If you are of youthful and/or of hormonal disposition, you and your friends might want to try a round of "I bet you can't do this," by which you see who can step into the full fury of the falls, while maintaining their composure.

MT. ROSE TRAIL

Plenty of switchbacks, all very steep and difficult. After a long, laborious climb, you break into some nice views along the loop circling the 4,300-foot summit.

Personally, I find the Mt. Ellinor trail shorter and easier to the top, with the views far better from there.

Mt. Rose is more of a fitness and cardio destination, a place to see what you can do.

MT. ROSE RECREATION AREA

Along the lakeshore here are picnic tables and little beachfront nooks created recently by Tacoma Power & Light, owners of the Lake Cushman Dam and all its megawatts of electricity.

They make perfect family picnic spots, where moms and dads can relax while keeping an eye on swimming children.

Sweaty, well-worked hikers returning from Mt. Rose will also appreciate the cool, refreshing water of Lake Cushman, which gets plenty warm in summer.

If you continue on toward the Staircase entrance to Olympic National Park, you will find plenty more places to picnic and swim along the lake. Some are heavenly spots with cliffs shaped perfectly for diving.

We'll cover these in the next chapter.

39/Lake Cushman Swimming Spots

DIRECTIONS

Taking Highway 119 westward 9.2 miles from Hoodsport, set your ODOMETER to zero at the road ending "T," then turn left toward Staircase. At 4.1 miles you are there. This rock outcrop has privacy, shade, soft spots for towels and sun bathing, plus two rocky knobs for jumping into the lake.

SEASONAL CONCERNS	ROAD CONDITIONS	TRAIL DIFFICULTY	SAFETY CONCERNS	TRAILHEAD PASS?
ALL SEASON	POTHOLES	EASY	PICNIC SAFE	NONE

Definitions of Terms: Pages 14-15

So much gets written and said about lovely Lake Cushman. So much of it is good press, and, indeed, so much of it is true.

- Clean, clear water
- Incredible mountain scenery
- Starts getting "Nordic" warm by May; near perfect swimming temperatures June through September
- Not too many boats or noise
- Lots of picnic spots and private, secluded beaches
- World class and world famous Party Rock with 20-foot jumping/diving height
- Access is FREE within the Lake Cushman Recreation Area
- Right next to Staircase, Olympic National Park, Mt. Rose, Mt. Ellinor

EVERYBODY KNOWS

Unfortunately, such good news travels far and wide. The one thing not normally spoken of are the enormous crowds that arrive all summer long to enjoy Lake Cushman's splendor.

Come, visit Lake Cushman! Swim in a gorgeous alpine lake!

However, dear readers, please consider a plan for beating the crowds. First off, can you visit on weekdays instead of weekends? Can you arrive no later than 10:00 a.m.?

This is serious business. Too many people drive for hours to visit Lake Cushman, only to sit in a long line of cars, miles from its shores, angry at the world for what is merely their fault for not preparing properly.

HEAVENLY LEDGES

So, while there's hardly a bad choice for where to put your blanket and go in the water, Lake Cushman offers some truly fine and special spots you ought to know about.

All the best ones have some type of rock and jumping features, shade trees and a degree of seclusion. These are all at the far end of the lake, one to two miles beyond the section of well-developed picnic spots near the Mt. Rose Trailhead.

My absolute favorite can handle up to three groups of swimmers. It has a flat area at the top of a huge boulder for coolers and shoes and such. It has cliffs on three sides, ranging from 4 to 8 feet over the water--perfect for kids of all ages.

Best of all, the water is clear so you can be sure of a safe jumping experience.

Lastly, if this spot is already taken--arrive at 9:00, I'm telling you!-- then just drive slowly and select the next available nook on the lake.

PARTY ROCK

Continue towards Staircase, reaching a section of road where rockslides have destabilized the hillside. Keep a lookout for a large rock just offshore in the lake; it will most likely have a rope attached to the top and show some wear-and-tear from many people climbing its surface.

Known by "Jumping Rock" and other names, it is also commonly referred to as the Party Rock for its choice as a location for spontaneous acts of youthful reverie, the particulars of which I do not want to go into here.

Youthful indulgence aside, the view of someone leaping from this boulder, with blue water and 4,000-foot mountains in the background, is a world-class image that has appeared in numerous video clips, social media and print publications. It is both a wonder to behold, and certainly a wonderful act to perform.

40/Shady Lane to Staircase

DIRECTIONS
From Hoodsport take Highway 119, going 9.2 miles where you'll end at a "T". Go left for another 5.4 miles, turning left to take the causeway bridge across Lake Cushman. From the turn it is exactly .7 miles to the parking area for both Shady Lane (right) and Copper Creek (left) trails.

SEASONAL CONCERNS	ROAD CONDITIONS	TRAIL DIFFICULTY	SAFETY CONCERNS	TRAILHEAD PASS?
ALL SEASON	POTHOLES	EASY	PICNIC SAFE	NONE

Definitions of Terms: Pages 14-15

As you cross the causeway bridge at the far end of Lake Cushman, you'll draw near to some of my all-time favorite trails and points of interest.

DRY CREEK TRAIL

Immediately on the other side of the bridge is a gated road bearing left. After that you'll see a signed parking area and restroom indicating the Dry Creek Trailhead. The Dry Creek Trail begins at the gated road.

After 1.5 miles, Dry Creek Trail begins its steady and fairly steep climb, eventually reaching more than 3,000 feet where it terminates at a logging road.

I want to make a short reference to the first part of this trail, which is all level and very well maintained: If you take it you will come across several inviting and secluded lakefront beaches, but these are all on private property except for the very last one, just before the trail begins its long ascent.

In fact, the entire first mile or so, the trail bisects one private property after another. You are basically hiking through a lot of back yards.

One odd benefit is that all these homes have been built "off the grid" in more ways than the fact they are not on a public utility. Here Northwest independent attitudes are expressed freely, and as you pass these hidden homes far up the lakeshore, you might want to note their unique methods of construction and problem-solving designs.

Keep a special eye out for the "Space Needle" home, which is a multi-sided, bright green treehouse built around a tall fir tree growing in its center. It is a work of genius, primitive art. It will not be hard to miss this beauty about a mile and a quarter down the trail.

SHADY LANE

Find Shady Lane Trailhead at .7 miles from the turnoff to cross Lake Cushman causeway bridge. It begins less than 100 yards after the sign (or signs) for Copper Creek Trail, another fabulous trail that we'll cover in the next chapter.

Shady Lane was missing its trailhead sign last time I was there. The trail might be a little hard to find, so look for the culvert crossing Copper Creek--with its signature red rocks--and be aware that the creek often runs dry.

Immediately beyond the culvert is a wide pullover for parking on your left, just below a giant, old growth cedar. The trailhead is on the other side of the road from here.

Park here for either Copper Creek or Shady Lane trails.

SECRETS OF SHADY LANE

Shady Lane has two special features. First, it is a back door into Staircase and the Olympic National Park, delivering you to the ranger station at Staircase itself in less than 1.3 miles, and at a cost of exactly zero dollars.

But for folks living on a tight budget, here is a nice way to think of the Olympic National Park's Staircase Loop Trail: an exquisitely beautiful 2.5-mile loop that you can top off with another beautiful 2.5 mile there-and-back on Shady Lane, saving your entry fee dollars for other worthy destinations on the Olympic Peninsula.

Much has already been written about Staircase Loop, by the way. Indeed, it is the Uno Primo family trail anywhere in this part of the Olympics. The Red Rock swimming hole is a summertime favorite with its 12-foot cliffs, as is the giant fallen cedar--bigger than a whale. Another favorite is the new and elegantly designed footbridge, a top picnic, swimsuit and international "be seen" location.

FOR THE TREES

The second "secret" of Shady Lane is that, after walking barely a quarter-mile from your car, you will come to a cathedral of giants--a large grove of nearly two dozen old growth cedars and firs. The trail passes right below them, passing through ancient logs cut to make the way for you. At other spots, you will stare up 20 feet to the top of an octopus-like giant root wad, the Hydra end of a massive, toppled evergreen.

Taking all these giant trees in with your eyes, assessing them, spinning underneath them and looking up over 200 feet into their branches, visually lining them up against your friends or family as you frame photos, locking hands and surrounding them, hugging them--all of these activities are your possible experience on Shady Lane Trail.

It is a well maintained, level trail all the way from the cathedral of giants to its end where it meets the Staircase Loop. However, it is boggy and muddy in places, especially after recent or lengthy rains.

Finally, the trail leads to a ledge and footbridge topping 30 feet above the North Fork Skokomish River. From here, you'll obtain breathtaking views up the Skokomish River Valley, as well as "box seats" for watching the hot summertime fun when lots of kids are swimming beneath you, one of the perks of the national park campground directly across the river.

You too can swim there if you like.

Supreme rendezvous spot, the new footbridge at the halfway point on Staircase Loop Trail.

41/Copper Creek Mines & Trail

DIRECTIONS
From Hoodsport take Highway 119, going 9.2 miles where you'll end at a "T". Go left for another 5.4 miles, turning left to take the causeway bridge across Lake Cushman. From the turn it is exactly .7 miles to the parking area for both Shady Lane (right) and Copper Creek (left) trails.

SEASONAL CONCERNS	ROAD CONDITIONS	TRAIL DIFFICULTY	SAFETY CONCERNS	TRAILHEAD PASS?
SNOWY TRAIL	DECENT ROAD	MODERATE/ DIFFICULT	MILD KID CAUTION	NONE

Definitions of Terms: Pages 14-15

Lovely Copper Creek Trail follows the original miners' route up the creek drainage first established around 1914. For a few brief years several mine shafts were blasted in this area, with eager owners hoping to find a motherlode of copper--as well as gold--based on the fairly promising traces of manganese and other minerals found nearby at the surface.

The Brown Mule Mine, which produced a single carload of copper ore during all of World War I before closing, still has four (and some say five) mine entrances near the Copper Creek Trailhead.

Families with young boys, in particular, might want to pack some headlamps or flashlights before hiking the trail. All four of the mine shafts are tall and wide enough to enter; they all go about 100 to 150 feet before ending in complete, TOTAL DARKNESS.

One of the two mines in the hillside above the first footbridge has a notable, hip-high step you must climb near the end, from which a tiny rivulet of water spills, making a creepy-sounding, classic wet echo, poink-poink-poink, that we've all heard in horror films.

In general, all four mines are of the damp dungeon variety, but do not pose any serious water hazards. Just puddles. You can make it to the end of all of them without getting your feet too wet.

FIND MINES

The first two mine shafts are located along the logging road where you park to take either Copper Creek or Shady Lane Trail. Somewhere between 100 to 200 feet further up the road from the giant cedar, start looking for a dark, square hole in the rock cliffs on your left.

The second shaft is also in the side of the cliffs, about 100 feet past the "Entering Olympic National Park" sign, which is itself about 400 yards uphill past the parking area. Both entrances, especially the second, slant down, so look just above ground to find them.

The next two shafts are black holes in the steep hillside above and across the creek. You must hike in about a third of a mile to find the first. It is visible from the first footbridge or the slight rise just before the bridge. A large tree came down a few years back and now partially obscures the entrance; both of these mine shafts are hard to find, especially the second one.

To find the second one, it is recommended you hike up another quarter mile, then turn and slowly come back down. You can find this entrance easier with a downward view.

TRAILS AND TRIBULATIONS

Much is made of Copper Creek Trail's steep ascent. Yes, it gets good and tough "on the back nine," as they say, but it is only a 2.1 mile haul to the top.

At 1.4 miles, you get the shaft. Look for the entrance to yet another mine, the Apex Mine, after a short branch. Retrace then ascend to the ridge crest separating Copper and Elk Creek watersheds. At 1.9 miles the trail branches again, with both branches leading to the ridge crest. A short connecting trail links these two branches, forming a loop.

Your reward for hard work is a nice view.

BEAUTY FIRST

The Copper Creek Trail is an artfully designed and landscaped trail, full of bridge-building and trail-making pride, thanks to the loving attentions of the Mt. Rose Trail Crew.

The trail does not gear up into its steeper portions until after .75 miles in. Prior to that, it is a gorgeous, moderate climb, full of clever steps, log obstacle solving and stump carving, distinct, efficient bridge work, and just pure fun as it stays close to the tumbling creek.

When the creek is running well, pull off trail to sit beside her on a sunny rock, overhanging ledge, or wooden bench built just for that purpose. There are pools and small waterfalls to play in. Great, great places to slip away, enjoy lunch or a bottle of wine, and take sensuous, rich photos of the mossy-clad trees and creek, full of red manganese rocks.

If the trail starts getting too steep for you, pace yourself and try setting the Apex Mine as your destination. Find it and win!

42/Alley Falls & Snow Lake Falls

DIRECTIONS

From Hoodsport take Highway 119, going 9.2 miles where you'll end at a "T". Go left for another 5.4 miles, turning left to take the causeway bridge across Lake Cushman. From the turn it is exactly .7 miles to Copper Creek Trailhead, where you will want to re-set your ODOMETER to zero.

SEASONAL CONCERNS	ROAD CONDITIONS	TRAIL DIFFICULTY	SAFETY CONCERNS	TRAILHEAD PASS?
SNOW LEVEL	4WD ROUGH ROAD	EASY	SAFE	NONE

*Definitions of Terms: Pages 14-15

Thank you, Stan Graham, for personally taking me to the following cool waterfalls, and for also, I have to admit, showing me those two mine shafts just off Forest Road #2451.

Now, this next adventure is for people who really like to tally their waterfalls and cross them off the list. These two sets of falls are not the most extraordinary, but they definitely qualify as bona fide watery wonders, though more on the scale of humble Watson Creek or Four Mile Falls.

With that understanding, let's get going. Do be aware, however, that the road you are about to take is one of the most challenging and breath-taking for being so high and fully unguarded.

Four-wheel drive? Yes!

Deep breaths and courage? Yes!

White knuckles on steering wheel? Perhaps.

DRIVING THERE

Let's pick up from where we left off in the previous chapter: the trailhead at Copper Creek.

Set your odometer to zero here.

You'll be staying on Forest Road #2451 the whole way, passing the entrance sign for Olympic National Park as you begin to climb along a steep mountain shoulder. At many places ahead the road will become crumbly and narrow, and the view out the passenger window will be of a 1,500-foot canyon wall dropping straight down.

If you've never done mountain road driving, this adventure will "build character," as my father used to say.

At 2.3 miles, away from any canyon edges, you'll come to a curve with a shoulder clearing on your left that is sometimes used for roadside camping. Note the very beautiful creek running beside this clearing. Anyone shooting video or photos and looking for that classic tumbling brook--this is your shot.

ALLEY FALLS

This is also the beginning of Alley Falls, a crooked alley of boulders and dislodged logs stacked such that the creek zigzags through a maze of 10-and-15-foot plunging falls that twist and turn and drop in stages.

The creek, so serene and idyllic beside the road where you park, soon pinches down into a jagged, rocky channel that stair-steps upward for hundreds of feet.

At the roadside campsite, pick up what is clearly a waterfall lover's trail, following it up and over downed trees, boulders and unburied human waste (warning!) parallel to the cataracts on your right. Alley Falls is a series of falls, no singular one of astounding beauty, but a fun pursuit as you scramble between each roaring section. For an extra bonus, enjoy a few old growth evergreens towering in your way.

SNOW LAKE FALLS

Continue driving past Alley Falls. At 2.8 miles, you'll come to the narrowest and most challenging portion of the road. The cliffs crumble constantly here, and the road is barely more than tire tracks over loose rock.

At exactly 3 miles, the road branches.

Bear right and drop down. For the next 3 miles you will continue to ride the high mountain shoulder with the Four Mile Creek drainage thousands of feet below. You'll encounter more sections of loose rock, but not as bad as the ones already in your rear view mirror.

About 6 miles in and you'll cross a strong-looking white wooden bridge. Made from big slabs of timber, it is the standout structure of your journey. I've heard it called the "cable bridge" because it's partly secured with buried logging cables on each end.

From the deck of the bridge, look left. You'll see the 70-foot main drop of Snow Lake Falls, which continues spilling below and beyond the bridge. Moving about, you can glimpse other, higher stages of the falls, but I would say 70 feet describes the main plunge.

Snow Lake Falls is both hard to photograph and hard to get near as well. She does not have a clear, cool pool or other places to play in. Like I said, this is one for those who want to cross a 70-footer off their list.

Both Alley and Snow Lake Falls are names I've chosen, by the way. "Alley" because of the tight jumble of boulders, and "Snow Lake" because the lake is nearby, though the falls may not be directly connected.

The road dead-ends in about a mile, but not before passing a few other, smaller falls (fuller and more dramatic in the early spring). One of them is very easy to climb, with lots of tiny pools and interesting climber's mazes to solve.

Finally, the road here supports a flourish of wild berries: strawberry, huckleberry, blueberry, salmon berry, thimble berry and blackberry (two kinds). We've timed it to find all of them in season.

Right: 70-foot Snow Lake Falls from the cable bridge.
Below: the jumble of cataracts known as Alley Falls.

From Top: Fern at Spider Lake; picnic spot just above last pool at top of Vincent Creek Falls; towering old growth greets hiker on Spider Lake Trail; morning shadow of High Steel Bridge arches across South Fork Skokomish River rapids, 376 feet below.

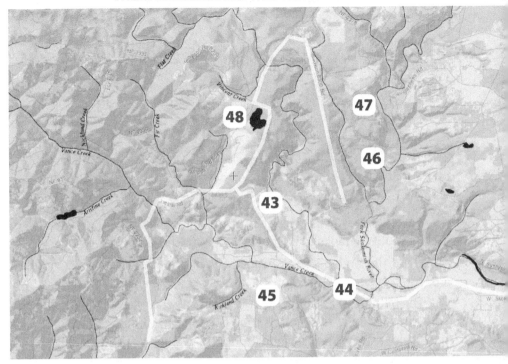

South Fork of the Skokomish Watershed

43. Vincent Creek Falls & High Steel Bridge . 114

44. Vance Creek Bridge **116**

45. Rock Creek Falls & Canyon............ **119**

46. Oxbow Campground & River Rafting ... **121**

47. Lower South Fork Skokomish

      Trail & Swimming Hole **124**

48. Spider Lake & Falls **128**

43/Vincent Creek Falls & High Steel Bridge

DIRECTIONS

From Highway 101 north of Shelton, turn left onto Skokomish Valley Road at the fish hatchery and intersection with Purdy Cutoff Road. Go 5.5 "country farm" miles until Forest Road #23 climbs to your right. Go 2.3 miles to the High Steel Bridge turnoff, making a right onto Forest Road #2340. Another 2.3 bumpy miles brings you to the bridge. For the falls, park on the near side, finding the trail on your left.

SEASONAL CONCERNS	ROAD CONDITIONS	TRAIL DIFFICULTY	SAFETY CONCERNS	TRAILHEAD PASS?
HIGH WATER	POTHOLES	SHORT MODERATE	CLIFFS	NONE

Definitions of Terms: Pages 14-15

Vincent Creek Falls attracts more eyeballs than any other waterfall in Mason County, thanks to its location next to the High Steel Bridge.

From the bridge deck, 375 feet above the Skokomish River, you get your best (and safest) view of the falls.

The falls are a stunningly beautiful site, a white, lacy highlight gushing from the side of a river gorge that is itself a 360-degree jaw-dropping masterpiece of nature. Without a doubt, the view from the High Steel Bridge is simply unforgettable.

At times the Skokomish snakes jade-green through the depths of the gorge, other times she roars milky white and churning with Class IV rapids while distant mountains are powdered with snow. Tall trees grow from the steep sides of the gorge. The bridge, massive in both length and height, seems a small, temporary thing made all the more fragile by the low, thigh-high guard rail standing between you and a 375-foot fall to infinity.

If you suffer from vertigo, stay far from the railings--the pull of gravity can seem overwhelming from such a sheer height. Over the years, numerous individuals have been killed or seriously injured by slipping off the deck railings or, more often, attempting to climb into the gorge for a below-the-bridge view.

Originally built by the Simpson Logging Company in 1929, the railroad ties and rails were removed and the bridge fitted with a paved surface when logging operations in this area ceased in the 1960s.

The bridge is a one-lane affair, with plenty of parking at both ends. Cross the bridge and park, looking for the short trail on your right which will lead to a viewpoint downstream where you may take photos of the bridge in context of its surroundings.

VINCENT CREEK FALLS

As stated elsewhere in this book, Vincent Creek Falls reigns as the tallest waterfall in this region of the Olympics. Simple math says the top of the falls are about 150 feet below the height of the bridge deck, so that leaves you 225 feet of falling water.

Viewed from the bridge, Vincent Creek horsetails 170 feet down, braiding into multiple white ribbons across the cliff face, then collecting in a pool before spilling another 60 feet into the river.

For those wanting to add another hour of thrills to an already thrilling site, consider a short trip down from the bridge deck to the top of the falls. Find the steep and very slippery access trail on the left side just before you reach the bridge you will see Vincent Creek about 150 feet below.

The trail, while not as dangerous as the many reckless approaches into the gorge itself, is still a challenge with sections of bare dirt and no handholds. It gets easier toward the bottom, and from there it is barely a hundred yards to your destination, the mystical top of Vincent Creek Falls.

By the way, the riparian zone here is gorgeous, full of berries and sorrel, a lemony, edible clover. The quality of light down here (something to do with the tree canopy overhead) makes for gorgeous "babbling brook" photos.

The mini-gorge just above the falls has a couple of nice wading pools, some mossy rocks for a picnic basket, and, in general, is a very cool, secluded hang out spot. It is also very safe, as you would nearly have to force yourself into the tight crevice where the water tumbles yet once more into another chasm before its final, vertical drop visible from the bridge.

Getting to this final ledge where the falls drops into the gorge--you can ponder how to get there, imagining a strong rope and harness, or some other safety measures, but I think this stunt is only for the crazy-brave.

Instead, enjoy the safe but rich pleasures of the wading pools at the top of Vincent Creek Falls.

High Steel Bridge photographed from near the top of Vincent Creek Falls.

44/Vance Creek Bridge

DIRECTIONS

From Highway 101 north of Shelton, turn left onto Skokomish Valley Road at the fish hatchery and intersection with Purdy Cutoff Road. Go 5.5 "country farm" miles until Forest Road #23 climbs to your right. At 2.3 miles you will pass the right-bearing turnoff for the High Steel Bridge. Continue on FR #23 for the next quarter mile or more, noting the large parking area on your left just after passing another forest road, also bearing left. Signs here indicate the trailhead for the Vance Creek Bridge.

SEASONAL CONCERNS	ROAD CONDITIONS	TRAIL DIFFICULTY	SAFETY CONCERNS	TRAILHEAD PASS?
ALL SEASON	POTHOLES	EASY	STAY OFF BRIDGE	NONE

Definitions of Terms: Pages 14-15

Tall, historic Vance Creek Bridge is the forbidden fruit of the Pacific Northwest. Every photo, every piece of publicity, every video and crooked selfie taken of it proclaim pretty clearly "Danger, Danger, Will Robinson!" but the hordes keep on coming.

Obviously, the chance to stand 347 feet high on an authentic railroad bridge built in 1929, with nothing to protect you from falling except your own common sense--this is simply too much freedom, too much raw reality to resist.

More than 800 feet long without a single safety rail, the bridge is undeniably a thing of both danger and beauty and certainly lives up to its status as a bucket list item for both world travelers and collectors of the bizarre.

Since 2012, thousands of images on Instagram and Google plus numerous articles on the web have drawn thrill seekers from all over the world to the Vance Creek Bridge. Every attempt to stop them has failed, including dropping trees across the trail, ripping up the railroad ties, wrapping razor wire around the foundations, and 24-hour security patrols handing out $150 trespassing citations.

So, here's what you'll need to know when you get there.

TRAIL AND BRIDGE CONDITIONS

Green Diamond Resource Company, owner of the bridge, actually wants you to view the bridge. They've put in an official parking lot with historical signs, recently cleared and leveled the .7 mile trail, and even punched out a short spur trail to the edge of the gorge so visitors can have a panoramic view of the span.

What Green Diamond--and their armed patrol officers--DON'T want you to do is to climb up on the bridge.

One more time: DO NOT CLIMB ONTO THE DECK OF THE BRIDGE.

The trail is wide, level and dry for most of its length; one gully, very near the end, requires that you scramble down and up, with a little stream you must jump across.

You'll see the spur viewing trail about a half mile in. After taking in the view, return the same way you came. What looks like a connector trail along the rim of the canyon is a complete disappointment, and will lead you into a wet mess when you reach a nasty part of the gully mentioned earlier.

From the main trail, however, once you scramble out of the gully, you come to the original foundation of the bridge. For some people, this one view is all they need: an enormous thrust of steel jutting out into space. For the first hundred feet just twin iron girders, knobby with rivets, no wider than a pair of diving boards.

Didn't I just tell you not to go on the bridge? Instagram pilgrim from Astoria, OR, makes his selfie dash to secure a memory and membership in the Vance Creek Bridge Club.

Then the rest of it, a rusted iron rainbow stretching 700 feet from canyon side to canyon side.

Your imagination takes over. Your intuition fires up. You can already taste the feeling of being out there and exposed, just by looking at the vast span. Your feet feel the call of the high wire act. Vance seems to talk to you, to taunt you.

"All the way from Ohio? You don't say, chickenshit."

This is the feeling of the universal inner dare. It's the dark lure. Your first cigarette. It's why so many people show up at the summit of Mt. Rainier, Mt. Everest, the edge of the Grand Canyon, the top of the Empire State Building, the ledge next to Niagra Falls.

But Vance is especially attractive, like young Brando, because he's so rugged, wild, and yes, forbidden fruit. Darn, that drives so many visitors wild that they ignore the warnings and their own common sense and decide to climb the foundation, push through the razor wire, balance while they plank walk along naked girders, then step across countless crumbling railroad ties to be out there on the Vance Creek Bridge, taking selfies and creating their own "I Stared Down Death" story to share with pals back home.

JUMPING TO CONCLUSIONS

Rumors have been sputtering like a spot fire that refuses to go out, rumors since 2014 that a bungee jumping company will either purchase or lease the bridge.

While the bungee idea seems anything but a foregone conclusion, a hard certainty is that Green Diamond would like to somehow be relieved of the constant liability and costs associated with the bridge.

"We're not in the amusement park business," says Patti Case, Green Diamond Resource Company public affairs and regulatory manager.

Unfortunately, with every new person who climbs up and walks out on the Vance Creek Bridge, the odds of an accident or unfortunate incident increase. That, in turn, could force Green Diamond to make a rash decision to dismantle the bridge.

Please do your part and stay off the bridge. Give Vance a chance.

45/Rock Creek Falls & Canyon

DIRECTIONS

From Highway 101 north of Shelton, turn left onto Skokomish Valley Road at the fish hatchery and intersection with Purdy Cutoff Road. Go 5.5 "country farm" miles until Forest Road #23 climbs to your right. SET ODOMETER. Stay on FR #23 for 2.5 pothole miles, then 3.1 paved miles (5.6 total) until you come to a steep canyon with a concrete guardrail on your right. Park after driving over the large Rock Creek culvert ahead, just past a closed, overgrown road on your left, using the wide parking area on the right.

SEASONAL CONCERNS	ROAD CONDITIONS	TRAIL DIFFICULTY	SAFETY CONCERNS	TRAILHEAD PASS?
HIGH WATER	POTHOLES	CANYON	CLIFFS SWIFT WATER	NONE

Definitions of Terms: Pages 14-15

Rock Creek flows out of the southernmost Olympics until it comes to Forest Road #23, where it passes under the road through a truck-sized smooth bottom culvert. There, at the final concrete inch of the culvert, it abruptly spills 30 feet over Rock Creek Falls.

Up to this point, Rock Creek has been fairly mild and placid, winding out of the hills with a few riffles here and there. But from the moment it drops into the pool below Rock Creek Falls, it surges at a breakneck pace, cascading more than 500 feet while squeezing through a bruising, unforgiving, half-mile canyon before spilling into the South Fork Skokomish River barely a mile above the High Steel Bridge.

I have studied the canyon from its rim along FR #23. It looks like a place you had better bring ropes, as well as someone with serious climbing experience. Catching an upstream angle while studying the canyon on Google Earth, I saw a singular waterfall that must be 50 feet or more.

The Rock Creek Canyon is on my "to do" list for 2019. I know for a fact it joins the Skokomish at a nice, fairly level junction, which, in turn, allows you to safely exit the river canyon another half mile downstream.

But between the falls and the river junction is the deepest, steepest canyon I've ever considered for canyoneering. Scout it for yourself from the guardrail along the gorge rim, and furthermore on Google Earth.

Unlike Lena Creek Canyon, this one seems safe enough to be feasible, and surely worth a try.

Meanwhile, Rock Creek Falls is another of those "checklist"

waterfalls that fall somewhat short of amazing. Obviously, coming out of a manmade culvert will take the shine off a waterfall's chrome, but if you start your exploration upstream of the culvert and walk back down inside of it, by the time you reach the top of the falls you will experience something "cinematic" in the way man and nature coexist. A huge wet tunnel turns into a falls.

Movie makers, consider this for an awesome scene in your video.

With low summer flows, you can climb down the falls. To photograph the falls from below, either climb down or go back to where I recommend you park, and find a short bushwhack trail that leads to the pool below.

30-foot Rock Creek Falls is the only other waterfall besides Lower Lilliwaup Falls to have concrete "bridge work" done to straighten its smile.

46/Oxbow Campground

DIRECTIONS

Set your ODOMETER the moment you turn off Highway 101 onto Skokomish Valley Road. The trailhead to Oxbow Campground is on your right exactly 14.3 miles from here. Remember to bear right on Forest Road #23 at 5.5 miles up the valley, then stay on FR #23 all the way.

SEASONAL CONCERNS	ROAD CONDITIONS	TRAIL DIFFICULTY	SAFETY CONCERNS	TRAILHEAD PASS?
HIGH WATER	POTHOLES	MODERATE RETURN	PICNIC SAFE	NONE

Definitions of Terms: Pages 14-15

I highly recommend Oxbow Campground for families of small children who love nature but can't expect their littles ones to hike a long distance.

It's also a perfect short hike for river lovers of any age at any time of year.

With the Oxbow, you can have a deep wilderness experience, children and all, and achieve it at the end of a one-mile, mostly downhill walk in the park. In fact, if your kids can peddle bikes or trikes and you have a wagon or cart you can pull, then you can be camping in style under the stars, for free, and be only 20 minutes from your car, if and when you finally need to get back to civilization.

How many places can promise that?

TOO GOOD TO BE TRUE

The name Oxbow came about because it describes the horseshoe shaped bend in the South Fork Skokomish River where the campground sits in the center, flanked on all sides (nearly) like a castle surrounded by a moat. Locals have known and loved this campground for decades, despite years of parental neglect by the National Forest Service, including recent efforts to cut off access, remove pit toilets and decommission other amenities.

For 2019 and going forward, bring a shovel and plan on burying the past behind you. Also bring a small stack of firewood and dry kindling, just in case.

Hopefully, that isn't enough to discourage you, because heaven awaits you after you lock your car and finish a half-mile descent on an old access road. You'll level out at the neck of the Oxbow, catching your first glimpse of the wide, sunny sandbar where soon you'll find campsites like the numbers 7,8,9,10 on the face of a clock, all the way to 5 along the shape of the bow.

These are beautiful, wild and well preserved sites, often with two or three separate nooks among the bushes for tents to tuck away, allowing kids, friends and parents their own privacy and special views.

Fire rings are generous, and at 10:00 on the bow, a large group fire pit can suffice for several campsites nearby. This area also serves as a flat, grassy commons for Frisbee games, sunbathing, badminton (I suppose) and group star gazing--which is way more fun, by the way, if you make up and name your own constellations.

Look for some cool, hidden sites at the 5:00 position; a couple of these hover on the rising bluffs just above where the river is carving a very deep swimming and jumping hole.

Though driftwood seems plentiful at the early part of the camping season, you can expect to walk (and work) a bit harder for firewood as the summer wanes. Bring a hand saw to cut limbs and branches from large, beached trees.

A RIVER RUNS ROUND IT

Remember, the earlier in the season, the higher and colder the river. By mid-summer the river runs pretty shallow and tame.

You'll find the hours go by as you walk the shores, ford from side to side, finding colored rocks, twisted driftwood and other treasures. The river's sound is soothing. In summer it's common to come across warm pockets of water, places where the river has dropped and left behind a shallow pool.

Absolute paradise! Warm water in the wilderness! By the way, you can channel and dam off your own warm water.

However, the number one favorite local pastime is to inflate rubber or plastic rafts, catching the Skokomish way upstream at 7:00 on the circle, then riding the rapids throughout every twist and turn, coming ashore at 5:00, only to cut across to run the gauntlet once again.

Around 11:00 and 12:00 there's a short set of breakers, probably a Class II, but most kids can handle the jostle if they have life vests on and adults nearby. Just watch closely and use your judgment, or arrange that they ride with you for safety.

ONE HILL OF A TIME

It is a little steep on your return, so plan accordingly. Remember, you've camped more than 400 feet below your car.

By the way, it's easy to drive right past the gated entrance to the campground, especially since the forest service took out the kiosk sign. I am sure their excuse for the neglect is that we citizens are making a mess for them, giving them too much work.

To this end, bury your stuff and pack out your trash. Show them who pays their wages, and show them you can keep it clean.

Beside a riverside fire pit at the Oxbow Campground, the Skokomish River cloudy and high in winter.

47/Lower South Fork Skokomish Trail and Swimming Hole

DIRECTIONS

From Highway 101 north of Shelton, turn onto Skokomish Valley Road at the intersection with Purdy Cutoff Road. Go 5.5 "country farm" miles until Forest Road #23 climbs to your right. SET ODOMETER. Take FR #23 until you come to where it branches uphill left, at 9.5 miles. Instead take FR #2353 downhill until you cross an old bridge, then bear left until you see the first of three trailheads.

SEASONAL CONCERNS	ROAD CONDITIONS	TRAIL DIFFICULTY	SAFETY CONCERNS	TRAILHEAD PASS?
HIGH WATER	POTHOLES 4WD	EASY TO MODERATE	WATER CROSSINGS	NONE AT #120 ENTRY

*Definitions of Terms: Pages 14-15

Die-hard hikers widely agree the Lower South Fork Skokomish Trail is one of the most under publicized and underrated trails in the entire Olympic National Forest. I strongly second that.

First off, it is mostly level and easy to follow for its entire 10.3-mile length, winding alongside the slow and meandering South Fork Skokomish River, gaining only 500 feet within that span.

Secondly, the trail wanders through what must be truly called an ancient forest--an Olympic river valley where the logger's ax did not fall. Not only are hikers constantly craning their necks to look up at old growth cedar, hemlock and fir, but many become somewhat speechless as they stare into the vast, primitive understory of a classic Northwest rainforest--deep woods of chest-high ferns, twisting red vine maple, weird mushrooms and massive, crumbling old growth nursery logs, luscious red thimble and yellow salmon berries, ripe, purple huckleberries, lichen draped trees and moss beds so thick and vast one swears he or she must be walking on another planet.

The trail accepts dirt bikes and horse riders as well. Several established, well-spaced campgrounds allow you to make a weekend or more of your adventure. If you choose, simply camp off-trail.

In summer, many camp upon the wide, flat pebbly banks of the river. You can sleep on soft beach sand and your fire, fed by ample driftwood, is safely far from brush and trees. All trace is erased once the river rises each winter.

RIVER SWIMMING VIRGINS NO MORE

Here is the third and, in my opinion, the very best reason for hiking the Lower South Fork Skokomish Trail.

A little more than a mile on the trail, you will come to a clear blue swimming hole of such allure and magnetic beauty that I dare you to continue hiking without at least considering the idea of a refreshing river dip.

Let me put it another way: If there ever was a swimming hole for "river dipping doubters" and the unconverted to cold-water ways, this place is the most appealing, safe-looking swimming hole you can ever introduce a virgin to.

I have brought many of the "unclean" here and they have all succumbed to the temptation, going in deep, losing their cold water virginity and loving it!

NORTHWEST WARM

The upper South Fork Skokomish River runs shallow through the summer, in many places only ankle deep. The water pulls slowly through the shallows, heated by sun and millions of hot, glimmering rocks.

This sun-warmed current feeds the deep, green-blue channel where you should try your swim. You'll see this spot when the trail opens up and affords you the first unobstructed view of the river.

Just before you obtain this view, you will first pass a few side-spur trails leading to wide floodplains of bleached river rock. Willows, alder and thick brush line the river banks. You'll hear the river moving.

Soon you'll come to the wide panorama of the river valley, viewing the river on your left before low hills, as well as a distinct, caramel colored clay bank jutting out into the water on your right.

The water looks deep and still before the bank. The trail appears to be heading straight for it. Possibly a large old growth evergreen lies on its side just downstream and across the river from the bank. It used to stand mightily at the very tip of the clay bank point, but, like many before, fell victim to erosion.

It might also have washed away, pulled by floods further down the river.

Trail workers have blocked access to the bank point, due to fears of more erosion. The main trail bypasses the bank.

Considering that the best spots for blankets and picnic gear are on the far shore anyway, it is recommended you cross the river downstream of the swimming hole, and walk up the other side. Likewise, more spur trails lead to the river a short distance beyond the swimming hole; the water is even more shallow here and makes an easier crossing.

GETTING THERE

There are three main trailheads for the Lower South Fork Skokomish Trail. The first is marked by a forest service kiosk sign and restroom on your left shortly after you cross the bridge over the river (directions below).

The first trailhead adds a half-mile or more of uphill walking to your trip.

If you continue on FR #2353, you will come to the LeBar Horse Camp trailhead for the hike. This second entrance is shorter and more level, and meets up with the first trail. Both trailheads require a NW Forest Pass.

A third and even further shortcut is on your left about a mile further up the same road, marked by a small #120 sign that is easy to miss. (If you had set your odometer at the turnoff for Forest Road #23, it should read 11 miles at this point.) Take this narrow road to the third, **non-pass** trailhead.

No matter which entrance you choose, your path will come to the end of the high ridge above the river. The trail turns sharply away, slanting down. You will know you are entering an ancient forest at this point-- the large, uniform presence of the trees, the sense of the land being wild, intelligent, patient and very old.

You'll drop into a deep, rich, wet basin after hiking around a fallen, massive tree that lies parallel to the trail. From this basin you'll drop quickly once more, via five switchbacks, to a gorgeous stream crossing-- many dogs and horses drink here--which marks the beginning of the valley floor.

The river is just ahead, with your view of the swimming hole only yards beyond the first spur trails.

If you plan on any extensive hiking of the Lower South Fork Skokomish, be aware that this trail becomes very muddy during periods of heavy rain.

Above: First glimpse of the South Fork Skokomish swimming hole, from just off the trail. Below: Approching from downstream on the opposite side.

48/Spider Lake & Falls

DIRECTIONS

From Highway 101, take Skokomish Valley Road about 5.5 miles to the "Y" cutoff where you climb Forest Road #23. Set ODOMETER. At 9.5 miles take FR #23 to the left, going another 8.2 miles and looking for a wide parking area on your left with a tiny wooden Spider Lake sign nailed 15 feet high on a tree--approximately 17.8 on your odometer. If you hit the FR #2350 junction, you've gone too far.

SEASONAL CONCERNS	ROAD CONDITIONS	TRAIL DIFFICULTY	SAFETY CONCERNS	TRAILHEAD PASS?
SNOW LEVEL	POTHOLES	EASY	SAFE	NONE

Definitions of Terms: Pages 14-15

Spider Lake is a tiny hidden outpost of tranquility. While it sits at 1,700 feet in elevation and is impractical to visit during snowy winters, at all other times you can drive any car to Spider Lake, understanding, of course, that a pothole is still a pothole and will jar your vehicle's frame and shocks, no matter what you drive.

Spider Lake was spared the logger's ax. Its lakeshore is a sanctuary for old growth cedar and fir. Tall giants will greet you at nearly every turn on the 2-mile loop trail. Bizarre, gnarly conks appear as white knobby steps along the sides of older, dying trees.

The trail dips up and down, undulating as it follows the contours of the lake. It makes an excellent jogging trail through a forest that is healthy, verdant, and full of life on every level. We heard fish jumping constantly but all we ever saw were rings on the surface where splashes had been.

Two wonderful solid log bridges make key stopping points on the trail. Each has a single handrail fashioned from tree branches, and wire mesh, for traction, stretched over the top of the log.

Spider Lake is a long, shallow lake that narrows in the middle. I've heard it warms in summer for swimming but have not swam there myself.

The lake level drops significantly as summer wears on, exposing clusters of half-cut, top-lopped trees--a bony armada of posts. They look similar to the old log mill posts still jutting from Hood Canal at Jorstad Creek, or the ghost tree trunks that reappear in Lake Cushman after the autumn dam releases are done.

You can swim and camp at several spots along the lake, but most of these are practically next to the main trail, so expect frequent company passing through.

For more room and privacy, find beautiful, hidden car camping at the end of rough, 4WD spur roads just past the main trailhead. Turn left onto Forest Road #2350 to find these.

In early summer Spider Lake Trail becomes berry heaven--or dare I say "berrydise"? Prepare to come home with purple-red hands.

Personally, I like to visit the lake in fall. Mist, fog, autumn colors and falling leaves--for me, Spider Lake is a moody, thoughtful, pensive place, a place of haunting, timeless beauty.

SPIDER FALLS

This waterfall will never make it on a postage stamp, not even a local post card. But it qualifies as one of 35 legitimate waterfalls in the greater Mason County area.

To find it, take Forest Road #2350 to the left just after the Spider Lake Trailhead. Go one half-mile, keeping an eye to your left. Spider Falls plunges about 35 feet in her final drop, splashing into a dead-end, rocky niche that hardly inspires further exploration.

Parking off-road is easy here. Step out to view the steep hillside above the falls, where you'll see higher tiers of falling water. This may or may not increase your respect, especially in the summer, when Spider Falls runs nearly dry.

A half-mile further down this road, you'll come to a big, old growth fir right beside the road shoulder. Note the sweet little creek running through the alder-rich valley on your right. The riparian zones in this part of the Olympics are famous for their logged, then unplanted recovery states; alder trees were allowed to take over, vastly influencing the wider ecology.

Another mile further on, you'll come to a bridge and a confluence of two sweet creeks. This is an amazing, beautiful car camping area, much loved by locals.

Spider Lake Falls, a humble tumble of white water hidden in a cleft just off the road. In summer she runs low to dry.

From Top: Woodpecker ambitions; sorrel salad bar, ready for picking.

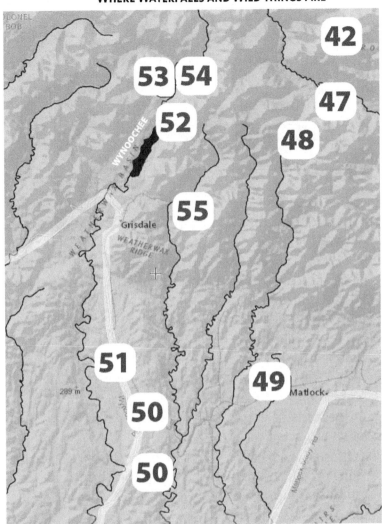

Wynoochee River Watershed

49. Truman Glick Park. 132
50. John Tornow Grave & Shootout Site . . 134
51. Ring of Fire Locomotive Wreck Site . . 138
52. Wynoochee River, Lake & Dam 141
53. Maidenhair Falls 143
54. Wynoochee Falls. 145
55. Spoon Creek Falls 147

49/Truman Glick Park

DIRECTIONS

Arriving in Matlock via Shelton-Matlock Road, you come to the 4-way intersection by the Matlock Store. Continue straight ahead on Deckerville Road, going 2.2 miles until you come to Ford Road. Make a right on Ford and go 1.2 miles until you see the park, with its chain link fence, on your left.

SEASONAL CONCERNS	ROAD CONDITIONS	TRAIL DIFFICULTY	SAFETY CONCERNS	TRAILHEAD PASS?
ALL SEASON	DECENT ROAD	EASY	PICNIC SAFE	NONE

Definitions of Terms: Pages 14-15

You might well argue that tiny Truman Glick County Park, without a ripple of water in its 36 acres, is hardly worthy of a chapter in a book devoted to waterfalls and wild things.

Quite true, nothing very wild about it. But what earns its mention is the fact that pretty, peaceful Truman Glick is located in Matlock, the very epicenter of wild in Mason County, for it is the home of the "Wild Man of the Wynoochee," fabled outlaw John Tornow, reputed killer of six armed men.

Tornow survived while being hunted for nearly two years in the Olympics, generating newspaper headlines throughout the world. His was the last true "Wild West" posse and gunfight to play out near Matlock in 1913.

Tornow's gravesite is near Truman Glick Park, as well as a museum housing some of his artifacts.

Matlock itself is the gateway to Tornow's kill site memorial, which is also near the "Ring of Fire" movie site where a burning locomotive fell in 1961 (and still remains) in the bottom of Wynoochee Canyon.

Nearby are beautiful Wynoochee Lake and four prominent waterfalls, including Spoon Creek Falls, where you can safely fall backwards, like the "trust game," into a swirling granite whirlpool.

PARK STATS

Truman Glick Park consists of land donated in 1978 and named for a supervisor, Truman "Bud" Glick, who used to work on the Simpson Logging Company railroad.

From the moment you turn into the park and drive to the parking area, you sense you are in a place much beloved. Locals hold weddings, parties and memorials on the wide, sweeping lawn.

A sturdy, well built covered picnic pavilion holds three large grilles, wash tubs, plenty of picnic tables and electrical outlets. Right next to it is a fabulous, super-padded kids' playground with lots of things to climb, hang, and swing on.

At the end of the large lawn stands the park's icon, a curved arch wooden bridge over lazy, little Decker Creek. Many a bride has crossed here with her maidens.

Decker Creek borders the large lawn and provides an inviting way for kids to interact with nature--stick forts, rock skipping, frog hunting, butterfly and small minnow catching, the whole gamut of games in a stream. Adults can play cards or sleep nearby on towels or blankets.

The park's trail system barely totals a mile, but with sweet, stately trails that meander and bisect each other, keeping any new hiker curious to the end.

This is a superb jogging park or place for quiet contemplation, whether walking wetland and wooded trails, or lying in the deep grass, listening to the creek while watching clouds loll by.

Arch bridge over slow, placid Decker Creek in Truman Glick County Park.

50/Outlaw John Tornow's Grave & Shootout Site

DIRECTIONS
Contained in the body of the chapter.

SEASONAL CONCERNS	ROAD CONDITIONS	TRAIL DIFFICULTY	SAFETY CONCERNS	TRAILHEAD PASS?
ALL SEASON	VARIES 4WD	EASY	SAFE	NONE

*Definitions of Terms: Pages 14-15

Several good books have already been written on John Tornow, the tragic outcast, outlaw and deep woods survivalist who killed six men before being killed as well in a final shootout in a swamp near the Wynoochee River.

We can only capture the briefest highlights of his story here. In my opinion, the best book written on him is called "Beast Man" by Mike Fredson. Fredson provides an insightful, well researched recounting of all the greed, family dysfunction, boiling anger and then, unfortunately, some critical underestimation of a very misunderstood loner who just happened to be a very good shot.

To put it mildly, there is much that happens before the powder keg incident where Tornow allegedly shot to death his twin nephews in 1911. Nevertheless, their murders light the fuse on an 18-month manhunt that includes a deputy and a tracker being murdered in a forest ambush, and then a final, blistering shootout where two other men fall to Tornow's deadly fire before he is killed by the only man to walk out alive from Tornow's swamp hideout that day.

HISTORICAL REGION

You can make a case for establishing a John Tornow Historical Region between Matlock and the Wynoochee River. You would begin with the aging Bauer Farmhouse, where his twin nephews' bodies were laid before their burial. There are also crumbling foundations of schools and other buildings that Tornow shared history with, as well as the old Grove Cemetery itself.

But the existing Matlock Museum, Tornow Gravesite and Wynoochee Shoutout Site are considered the top three stops for those attracted to Tornow's legend. Including time spent in your car, you can visit all three locations in three to four hours.

DIRECTIONS

Get on Shelton-Matlock Road by taking the Matlock/City Center exit from Highway 101 in Shelton, heading for Matlock. You can also pick up Shelton-Matlock Road by exiting Highway 101 at Dayton-Airport Road, which is Highway 102.

You'll pass through Lake Nahwatzel on the way to Matlock. The resort and restaurant have been reopened and I highly recommend you try this establishment for a meal.

At the main intersection in Matlock (at the post office and general store) you'll want to set your ODOMETER.

Turn left onto Matlock-Brady Road, going three miles to Mary M. Knight School. Immediately past the school you will see the Matlock Museum on your left.

Open hours are very minimal here. The only certain time is the first full Saturday and Sunday of May, which are the days of the annual Matlock Old Timer's Fair, the biggest--and most authentic historical--festival of its kind in the area. (Tornow fans and fanatics walk among visitors during the Old Timer's Fair; this is a great time to seek out their booth showcasing historic photos, trinkets, T-shirts and coffee mugs with Tornow's name on them.)

Continue on for 5.3 miles, arriving at the Grove Cemetery, on your right, exactly when you reach milepost 25. Tornow's grave is to the left of the flag pole. It is often adorned with empty cans of beer, empty pints of whisky, shotgun shells, handwritten poems, coins and the occasional marijuana cigarette.

Please note the other Tornow family headstones, and how near their death dates are to John's. The Bauer Twins lie only a few yards away, as does their mother's grave.

KILL SITE

From the cemetery, continue barely .2 miles to the Boundary Cutoff Road, where you'll turn right. When you reach Boundary Road in .3 miles, turn right once more.

Go past Tornow Drive (at 10.9 miles) and look for Cougar-Smith Road at 12.6 miles, where you will make a left and cross the Middle Fork

Satsop River.

Continue on Cougar-Smith, eventually crossing the Satsop again, where the road will turn into a gravel, private logging road for about two miles. At 18.1 miles you will come to a "T" where you want to turn right and head toward the Wynoochee Dam and Lake.

This is a beautiful paved road. Make nice time but start slowing down after you pass milepost 26. About .75 of mile and you will hit two portions of the road bordered by a metal guardrail on both sides. Just after the second pair of guardrails, the shootout site (or "kill site") comes up quickly as a small dirt turnoff that ends at a stump marked with a blue cross.

More often than not, you will miss this turnoff. It's just a tiny clearing that fits a few cars. If you've gone too far, you'll see milepost 27 on your right. Directly across from the sign is a small paved drive where you can turn around and go back to the turnoff.

TORNOW TRAIL

The trail to the kill site follows the edge of the logged parcel bordering the road, then angles into the woods another 200 yards before reaching the rock-and-mortar monument erected in 2014--marking a hundred years after the fateful fight.

Currently, many small altars and offerings have been built out of trees, stumps and other objects nearby. The entire scene is a holy, somber one, and reminds me of a pagan version of the Catholic "Stations of the Cross," a series of remembrances dedicated to the life and legend of a most unusual man.

This tour is excellent for the Halloween season and could also include the nearby "Ring of Fire" locomotive excursion described in the following chapter.

Above: You could do worse than hide in the treeline on Halloween night to see who shows up at John Tornow's gravestone, right. Below: Tornow historian and survivalist Dana Anderson with wife, Faaea. Anderson has done much to promote the Tornow legend, including a major role in bulding the shootout memorial.

51 / Ring of Fire Locomotive Wreck

DIRECTIONS

Find the locomotive by means of Wynoochee Valley Road (FR #22 originating in Montesano, WA). Pick up detailed directions in the body of this chapter.

SEASONAL CONCERNS	ROAD CONDITIONS	TRAIL DIFFICULTY	SAFETY CONCERNS	TRAILHEAD PASS?
SNOW LEVEL	VARIES 4WD	SHORT BUSHWHACK	CLIFFS KID CAUTION	NONE

*Definitions of Terms: Pages 14–15

Every year Shelton holds an annual screening of "Ring of Fire," a very modest, linear film made in 1961. Starring David Janssen and Frank "The Riddler" Gorshin, the film's climax centers on frightened townsfolk escaping a raging fire, wherein a burning railroad trestle collapses, sending a locomotive plummeting 200 feet into a gorge.

This famous scene was filmed over the Wynoochee River, about 30 miles from Shelton. Because many Mason County residents played roles as extras or were involved with other aspects of the film, you could say "Ring of Fire" has retained a strong loco appeal.

RAILROADING US

Well, Hollywood came and Hollywood left, and nothing was ever done to retrieve the broken locomotive. Think of it as the biggest Bud Light can you will ever come across in a river gorge.

The good news is that it's located barely two miles past the John Tornow shootout site and, in a similar fashion, remains a popular cult destination for fans of the movie (or fans of those who were in it).

To find it, continue on Wynoochee Valley Road towards Wynoochee Dam and Lake. Somewhere around milepost 28 you will see a sign for Save Creek. Set (or reset) your odometer as you cross the creek.

Within .2 of a mile, the woods on your left will open to a bare, fresh-cut swatch of land. A gated logging road borders the swatch, with an 0-600 sign posted on your left. It's the more common, but longer, way to the train. Just make note of 0-600 for now. Don't turn but keep driving.

Just short of a mile from Save Creek, you will see the next prominent logging road entrance on your left. Currently it is not gated. If not, you may try driving the first mile of the next set of directions. The road may be fine for any type of vehicle, but was under snow when I visited.

From this second entrance, this hike clocks in around 1.2 miles. The

0-600 entrance I mentioned earlier also goes to the locomotive, but is longer at 2.3 miles. However, it is more reliable and does not involve the off-trail bushwhack I am about to describe. It is the safer, sure route.

WHERE TO BEAR

Within a few feet the second logging road immediately branches. Take the right branch. A piece of orange tape will help you decide. You now pass through a young, planted alder forest. Then you head back into young evergreens for maybe .2 miles until you come to a large, distinguishable "Y" branch in the road. Bear right, checking for orange tape on the right side as confirmation.

In another quarter-mile this road dead-ends at a small circle. (Orange tape is your guide every step of the way.) Between 1:00 and 2:00, go over or around a brush pile and look for a high spot to view the valley below.

Look for a pair of old lightning-strike trees that were never logged, the tallest about 30 feet. They guard this hillside, heads above their much younger, commercial "offspring." You will use them as your return-trip site line from the bottom of the hill you are about to descend.

Look west toward the mountains. If you are in the right place, you will see another logging road only a hundred feet below you, but at a slope distance of maybe 300 yards. A critical feature of this road is the "Y" branch that should be visible just before the road winds out of sight. You're going to wind up there, bearing left for the final .3 miles to the gorge trail.

Pick up the orange tape trail below the two old trees. Drop down to the nearest point on the road, watching your step constantly for snags and collapsing logs. It gets very swampy just before the road. Use care crossing the bog--follow orange tape.

Once on the lower road, bear left and avoid the first open area with another right-bearing branch; this is not quite the access yet. About 400 yards further is the next parking area with your trail on the left.

The trail drops 60 feet into a fern-filled, boggy basin, then drops suddenly and sheerly over a rock ledge affixed with a safety rope. Use it. You'll end up on the viewing ledge, facing 200 feet of bone-crushing space if you slip any further.

The locomotive is mostly submerged in water, with green-blue riffles combing over its wheels. The passenger cars lie crumpled on the side of the gorge, huge rusty things that are nearly impossible to take pictures of without serious risk of falling. Photographer Larry Workman has captured romantic, dreamy images of the entire wreck--hats off to Larry--best of all, his shots were taken from down in the gorge.

The perch is pretty dramatic, however, with scenic, heart-stopping views of the Wynoochee's rapids, deep blue pools, and sheer cliffs as far as the eye can see.

You can sit and rest your back safely against the rope ledge, with room for a well-earned backpack lunch between friends. A faint trail leads to the left along the canyon ledges, however, I did not explore it and cannot say whether it provides a safe route down. It did not look likely. Please be careful up here.

A very nice place for a rope is the final ledge you drop over to reach the viewing perch above the locomotive wreck in the Wynoochee Gorge. Snow is visible along the river's shore 200 feet below.

52/Wynoochee River, Lake & Dam

DIRECTIONS

Follow the same directions as to the "Ring of Fire" locomotive in the previous chapter, or, alternatively, travel to Montesano, where you can pick up the Wynoochee Valley Road and take it some 30+ miles to the lake and dam area (a few miles past the historic Camp Grisdale sign marking where the last logging camp in America once flourished).

Turn left on Donkey Creek for the dam, public beach and Coho Campground. From that access, bear left on Forest Road #22 before reaching the campground and you will wind down to the fish ladder. For awesome river camping, continue straight on Wynoochee Valley Road until it becomes unpaved and signed as FR #2270. After a mile or more you will begin to get glimpses of the river and potential campsites on your left. A well loved cluster of beachfront campsites are just across a bridge and popular swimming hole six miles up the road.

SEASONAL CONCERNS	ROAD CONDITIONS	TRAIL DIFFICULTY	SAFETY CONCERNS	TRAILHEAD PASS?
SNOW LEVEL	POTHOLES 4WD	EASY	SAFE	NONE

Definitions of Terms: Pages 14-15

The Wynoochee River is one of the longest rivers to flow from the Olympic Mountains. Clear and cold, it snakes in a general southward direction until joining the powerful Chehalis River, Washington's second largest river (after the Columbia). From high in the mountains, she jumps and splashes down a rocky, zigzag course, but amazingly holds up and restrains herself for several miles after her show stopping performance at Wynoochee Falls. Though she bucks and rocks over a few more sets of rapids, in general she glides easily all the way to her manmade transformation as Wynoochee Lake, establishing a stretch of perhaps six miles above the lake that plays host to some of the best dispersed river camping anywhere in Olympic National Forest.

The numerous little side roads and "punch out" spots in the riverside foliage tell you that many, many locals have found their slice of heaven by camping on the Wynoochee--and there's no good reason you shouldn't join them.

So, riverside camping is one good reason for visiting the Wynoochee Recreation Area.

Number Two reason is all the waterfalls, especially the large, swimmable waterfalls. Host to three of the most dramatic (and most visited) waterfalls on the Olympic Peninsula, it is amazing that an 80-foot multi-tiered tumbler of a falls hardly gets a notice out here. This is a tall, sinewy beauty and would qualify as a big deal anywhere else in the Olympics, but is known commonly as "No Name Falls," because everyone who passes her--right beside the road, like Cushman Falls--is on their way to the much finer Wynoochee Falls.

WYNOOCHEE LAKE

Everyone loves Wynoochee Lake. Wynoochee Lake and Dam make the Goldilocks "just right" fit for a mountain-encircled, deep blue lake, big enough to hold small fishing boats, but small enough so the buoy-line protected swimming area (with imported beach sand) is just above the dam itself.

Fabulous, super-popular Coho Campground stays full all summer, with happy campers having nothing to do but swim, hike world-class trails, jump off waterfalls, and feast and party around the campfire with friends every night.

Tough life, eh?

The Wynoochee Lakeshore Trail, by the way, is a first-class, level, SUPERnatural trail full of old growth wonders, one of only four National Recreation Trails in the Olympic National Forest.

The old, venerable dam has a visitor center at Vista Point with viewing platforms that allow you to take in a massive, concrete dam that no longer produces electricity. Lots of photos and textual explanations help you understand the early 1900s white male mindset that felt driven to **conquer** the wild Wynoochee.

Be sure to glimpse down the gorge at the base of the dam. Such a tight, deep, narrow channel! For the next several miles, the Wynoochee River cuts through some of the deepest and most dramatic basalt canyons, such as the gorge where the "Ring of Fire" locomotive met its fate in the previous chapter.

If you are curious to see more of this amazing gorge, take Forest Road #22 down to the Wynoochee Fish Ladder (below the dam) to get a sense of what kind of terrain the Wynoochee cuts through.

Finally, after leaving the national forest, the Wynoochee shows her mellow side as she settles down and meanders slowly over the plains and wide river valley, coursing through placid farmlands, pastures and beside old baptist churches.

53/Maidenhair Falls

DIRECTIONS

Arrive at Lake Wynoochee by any means you choose. Continue straight to where Forest Road #2270 is first signed and the road becomes unpaved. Drive six bumpy miles to the gated entrance signed National Forest Cooperative Management Zone. Within a hundred feet you'll see a bridge crossing the Wynoochee River on your left. Take it.

Note the swimming hole to your right and campsites on the other side of the river. Once across the bridge, take the first left down a rough access road leading to several riverside campsites. About 200 yards or so, you'll come to a wide, circular parking area, with more campsites and smaller access roads branching out like spokes from a wheel.

A spur trail to the falls can be found here, on the woodsy side away from the river. If you don't find it, go back to where you first turned after crossing the bridge, and you'll see another spur trailhead there. The main trail is wide, groomed and parallels the river downstream.

SEASONAL CONCERNS	ROAD CONDITIONS	TRAIL DIFFICULTY	SAFETY CONCERNS	TRAILHEAD PASS?
FALLS DIMINISH	POTHOLES 4WD	EASY	MILD KID CAUTION	NONE

Definitions of Terms: Pages 14-15

Maidenhair isn't just a waterfall. It's an experience.

It starts with the trail, which is superb, unbelievably beautiful. This is part of the Lake Wynoochee Shore Trail System, a National Scenic Trail. On it you will pass beneath some of the most profound and gigantic old growth Douglas firs anywhere in the Olympics. The Maidenhair Falls Trail has moments every bit as dramatic as Shady Lane, Staircase Loop and Spider Lake--big, stately evergreens leaning out over the trail, all with tiny paths worn around their trunks from people visiting, touching and hugging them.

It's just under a mile to the falls. An easy, level mile. In late April we snacked on luscious green sorrel, with their arrow-shaped clover-type leaves covering the forest floor. Sorrel has a sour crabapple taste. Single trilliums bowed their white heads along the trail, and the pink budded salmon berries proclaimed spring stepping into high gear.

A half mile in and you begin to hear the falls. You're still near the Wynoochee River, however, and the two moving waters mix and play stereophonic games with your ears. Is that the river? Is that the falls? Now and then you'll glimpse shiny river rock glimmering through alder leaves.

Eventually you leave the river as the path rises in gentle curves, and soon you hear a new source of rushing water somewhere ahead. The land rises on the right and the trees loom their largest. You glide along a deep, wide stretch of ancient forest.

PAUL SIMON, THIS IS YOUR BRIDGE

I kid you not, if there ever was a bridge over troubled water, the footbridge crossing Maidenhair Falls earns the title.

You arrive at the bridge only after the roar of the falls has you follow several side-trails to the cliff edge for an overview. Sadly, these glimpses do not reveal the falls, only tease and heighten your expectations.

Finally, at the last overlook, you recognize the true nature of the falls; no sublime maidenhair or bridal veil falls here, but rather a torrential thunderbolt of liquid lightning smashing through a chasm.

The falls starts as a clear, strong stream pinching through the top of a narrow ravine, then roaring ten feet into its first churning bowl. It surges beneath an ancient, leaning cedar, rumbles under the bridge, then drops, foamy, two more times over five-foot ledges. This is canoe-crushing force, terrible water that suddenly drops into a violent, final churn so turgid that it pulses the air in waves you can feel on your skin-- whump, whump as water hammers rock.

Now, after all that, Maidenhair drops a final 30 feet or so into a sleek slot canyon, where it rolls out, placid as a lamb, to join the Wynoochee River a hundred feet beyond. (Another great reason for camping along the river is approaching Maidenhair Falls after climbing out of your inner tube.)

Despite my dramatic, purple-prose description, there are plenty of safe viewpoints from which to eat lunch and enjoy the falls. You simply want to stay OUT of this particular waterfall. However, the entire area retains its magic and begs for more exploration, with the trail continuing on toward Wynoochee Lake.

Bridge over Maidenhair Falls, which roars through a dangerous chasm. Plenty of safe, picnic spots nearby, however.

54/Wynoochee Falls

DIRECTIONS

Back Way: From Highway 101, take Shelton-Matlock Road to Matlock, going straight at the Matlock General Store four-way intersection. Proceed almost nine miles on Boundary Road, turning right on Cougar-Smith Road, crossing the first of two river bridges, then going the last 2.5 miles on unpaved private forest road until it ends at a "T" on Wynoochee Valley Road. Go right. Stay on Wynoochee Valley all the way until it becomes unpaved and changes to Forest Road #2270.

Wynoochee Falls is 8.2 miles of dusty, bumpy, 4WD forest road straight ahead. Look for the wide, round parking area with an old stone wall (a former sign) in the center. About a mile or so before the falls, you will pass beautiful, dramatic No Name Falls, splashing off the cliffs on your right. Regular Way: Take US Highway 12 to Montesano in Grays Harbor County. Pick up the Wynoochee Valley Road by means of signs for the Wynoochee Recreation Area.

SEASONAL CONCERNS	ROAD CONDITIONS	TRAIL DIFFICULTY	SAFETY CONCERNS	TRAILHEAD PASS?
FALLS DIMINISH	POTHOLES 4WD	SHORT & EASY	PICNIC SAFE	NONE

Definitions of Terms: Pages 14-15

One glance at Wynoochee Falls and you will know this is sacred land, a blessed gathering spot for tribes, hunters and fishermen going back thousands of years. While there are no official signs declaring such, you can feel it in the way the massive cliff dome dominates the deep blue pool.

When winter's waters rise, the Wynoochee pour over the wide breadth of the dome, stretching 60 feet or more, a roaring, white curtain of water, thundering as it churns the pool below.

In the summer, the falls narrow to cut a chute through sheer rock where they've been cutting for eons. Huge trees have fallen and locked onto each other in this chute--so deeply recessed it's almost a cave-- further obscuring the white foam of falling water. And even though she's restrained and hidden in her rock-cutting chute, Wynoochee Falls still pours a great deal of water 45 feet down.

GETTING THERE

From where you park after 8.2 miles on FR #2270, take the quarter-mile downhill trail that leads to the huge swimming pool where you'll face the falls. Note the 700-year-old, 200-foot-tall monster tree to your left. Note the other old growth giants.

During high water, you will see the wide, powerful falls. You won't be able to move along the shore very well, as the full pool will limit your mobility.

If here during low water and high temperatures, the pool will be idealistically shallow along the right side, allowing families and kids to frolic and thrive. The rock outcropping to the left of the falls becomes a beach and picnic grounds. Where the outcropping rises toward the falls, the ledge forms a popular six-foot jumping and diving spot.

As the pool narrows and runs off to become a river again, the water passes through a fairly deep channel formed by the mossy bluffs below the 700-year-old Douglas fir. This is also a very cool spot for jumping, swimming and fooling around.

However, no matter where you choose to swim or wade--the water is not freezing but still fairly cold--the Wynoochee Falls' broad, granite face dominates the scene, a towering brow 45 feet above the pool. You can see scoops and channels where winter's water carves her face. The granite gleams in daylight and you can climb this rock face easily to stand at the very lip of the falls.

You'll enjoy great, heart-pounding views here, fabulous photos, and, if you work your way down and towards the spilling chasm, you'll find several perches where local teens and wild elders leap 30 feet into the blue-green bowl below.

Arrive early and take photos drenched in dawn's golden light. You'll want to be here by 10:30 anyway if you plan on getting the best beach towel locations on the flat rock across the pool. Once crowds arrive, it is common to have 40 to 60 people swimming here.

Powerful Wynoochee Falls cuts through rock while old growth trees collect to form a roof over her summertime spill. In winter, the falls roar over the entire width of her face, in right of photo.

55/ Spoon Creek Falls

DIRECTIONS
Found in paragraph 2. Note that near milepost 32 of the Wynoochee Valley Road you'll pass the site of former Camp Grisdale, the last fully functional logging camp to operate in America, until 1985. Slow to find the abandoned mailboxes near a commemorative plaque where the ashes and spirit of Leon Keith Byrd reside, who served as Grisdale's maintenance supervisor for 18 years.

SEASONAL CONCERNS	ROAD CONDITIONS	TRAIL DIFFICULTY	SAFETY CONCERNS	TRAILHEAD PASS?
FALLS DIMINISH	4WD	SHORT EASY- MODERATE	PICNIC SAFE	NONE

Definitions of Terms: Pages 14-15

Spoon Creek Falls affords you a supreme outdoor thrill. With water temperatures warm enough for swimming, in summer you can paddle around an exquisite swimming hole, 100 by 80 feet, and to maximize your memory-making experience, you may climb the cliffs at the base of the falls to turn and face your companions before LETTING GO and falling backward into a natural, swirling Jacuzzi tub.

You find Spoon Creek Falls by going all the way back to the Wynoochee Valley Road - Donkey Creek intersection (near Coho Campground and the dam), and looking for the sign indicating Forest Road #23 in the opposite direction (right) of Donkey Creek. Follow FR #23 for 2.5 miles, crossing a 120-foot-high narrow bridge just before you park for the falls (clearly signed) on your right.

WINTER FALLS

Arrive in winter, and at the trailhead you can hear the falls roar. Just after you poke into the woods, a faint sub-trail leads left and allows you to stand directly over the 80-foot straight plunge of the falls. The swollen waters pound the rock "whirlpool" tub on the lower shelf, hitting with such force and volume that the stream explodes straight back in splashes 25-feet high.

No exaggerating; you can feel the falls pulsing in your feet as you stand on the precipice above. Beware, no more than 14 inches of dirt trail separate you from a fall to certain death.

Return to the main trail and follow a little further until a second left branch takes you to a safer overlook with a railing. You can watch the falls pulse against the rock here, however, photos are still far from ideal; you are not distant enough for good composition or proportion.

Unfortunately, that is all you can expect during times of high water. If you take the trail all the way to the bottom, Spoon Creek will most likely be running too high for you to approach the falls from there--unless you come prepared to walk upstream against a deep, strong and cold current.

SUMMER VERSION

In summer, Spoon Creek Falls shows a kinder, gentler side of herself. The trail is about a quarter-mile, all downhill, with the last stretch going in and out of her much-reduced streamflow as she comes into view.

Tall and straight, Spoon Creek spills into a whirlpool tub that can be attained by crossing her large, round swimming hole first, then climbing the wet ledge on the left side--although you can get there by the right-side approach, too.

When her water level is still high, May and June, the whirlpool plunge experience is a solid "10," with the tub being eight feet deep and so slick on the sides that you tumble like an egg in boiling--but cold--water. Once you drop in, you are rolled and roiled by pounding, bubbling waters, and you will come out fresh, renewed, and feeling like all your atoms have been scattered, reassembled and recharged.

As the falls' power wanes, the whirlpool level drops, and so does the force of her swirling action. It's still pretty good in late August, but not quite the same zest.

The main pool stays pretty consistently about five feet deep, and you can wade or swim to the falls. The water gets warmer than Rocky Brook Falls with plenty of direct sun.

At the approach end, you'll find a small beach and dry, rocky area for bags, clothes, and semi-standing as you drink or snack. You might be a little close to other company, as this is a popular spot on hot days. Downstream, your kids will find other attractions once they tire of the falls and swimming hole; Spoon Creek is full of rocks, frogs and crayfish, a veritable "hands on" aquarium and petting zoo.

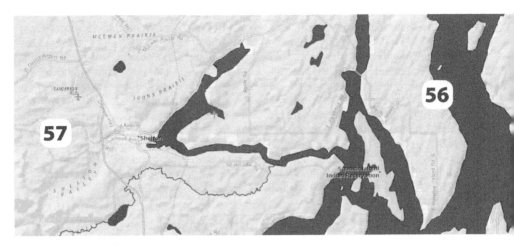

Other Wild Places of Interest

56. Fudge Point Beach **150**
57. Goldsborough Creek Otterfalls **152**
58. Essay: Waterfall Witness
Protection Program **155**

Goldsborough Creek

56/Fudge Point Beach

DIRECTIONS

Reach Harstine Island by means of State Route 3 between Belfair and Shelton. From Route 3, turn onto East Pickering Road and follow for several miles until you cross the Harstine Island Bridge. Bear left onto East North Island Drive, going 3.2 miles to the four-way intersection at the Harstine Island Community Club. Make a right, going several miles on E. Harstine Island Road, passing Appaloosa Drive before reaching E. Ballow Road, where you turn left. Go one mile until you come to a sharp left curve. A clear-cut field is on your right and two gates block dirt roads leading to the right just before you would complete the curve. Park here on the dirt clear spots just off the road shoulder. Take the upper, silver gate and walk .75 miles straight on this gravel road until you come to an intersection with a street sign (a short female name, forgotten). Turn left and go another .75 miles until this road forks above the bluffs over the beach. Take either fork (left preferred) down to the beach.

SEASONAL CONCERNS	ROAD CONDITIONS	TRAIL DIFFICULTY	SAFETY CONCERNS	TRAILHEAD PASS?
ALL SEASON	DECENT ROAD	EASY	PICNIC SAFE	NONE

Definitions of Terms: Pages 14-15

Lovely Fudge Point State Park is a park-in-progress, without anything built on it yet. It is located on the east-facing shore of Harstine Island and is naturally blessed with a half-mile of pristine, uninterrupted shoreline featuring melt-your-heart views of Mt. Rainier.

The land has been purchased and set aside for big, big things ("to be the finest jewel in the state park system,") however, the chronic financial woes of Washington State Parks is sure to delay any serious fashioning of Fudge Point into a recreational jewel.

Currently, its location has been so officially "downplayed" that you could say it remains in top secret status--or, more correctly, hidden in plain sight.

Well, not anymore, if you are reading this.

Despite the fact that a few state park employees will have to share their private beach getaway with a few of their tax-paying "employers," it will be good for ALL if a few more citizens can avail themselves of the fabulous, undeveloped natural amenities of Fudge Point. After all, more people can sound the drum for more attention--and financial support-- to go towards making this park a fully functioning reality.

John Muir plus Teddy Roosevelt equals Yosemite. Sometimes that's what it takes to get a good park started.

Driftwood collects along the narrow spit sheltering a cove at Fudge Point State Park.

LOOKING FORWARD

So, once you've made the drive and committed your time, what does Fudge Point have to offer you?

First, it's a good length hike for both kids and adults--three miles round trip--with a slight drop as you near the beach. You're on a wide, smooth gravel road the entire way, a forested "cake walk."

Second, it's berry heaven in summertime. You can eat your way to the beach. Be advised, however, that I have combed the woods on both sides and found no edible mushrooms at all.

Third, the shoreline is fantastic. Allowing a half hour to reach it with kids in tow--bikes and wagons are perfect for this journey--you will delight in the wide, pebbly beach that becomes sandy in spots, gently sloping and with no obstacles, trash or litter.

Stroll the beach northward to a sheltered cove, a tidal pond protected by a curving bank of sand. This is free parking for driftwood, with countless pieces laced together.

Facing distant homes on Longbranch Peninsula, the wide open sea channel sweeps up sounds and magnifies them, creating the low buzz of what I call "civilized silence."

Here's a common phenomenon of Puget Sound beaches: you can speak in whispers and hear the wind brushing your face. Yet at the same time you will notice the low constant rumble of Interstate 5 or the muffled climb of a SeaTac jet piercing the sky.

Fudge Point is wild enough to present the illusion that you are far from civilization. In truth, you are peering at its shores, still lovely nonetheless.

57/Goldsborough Creek Otterfalls

DIRECTIONS

Provided within chapter. This is technically private property and permission should be sought to visit the swimming hole.

SEASONAL CONCERNS	ROAD CONDITIONS	TRAIL DIFFICULTY	SAFETY CONCERNS	TRAILHEAD PASS?
HIGH WATER	DECENT ROAD	LONG BUT EASY	WATER CROSSINGS	NONE

Definitions of Terms: Pages 14-15

After decades of hauling millions of board feet of timber on its private railroad into downtown Shelton, in 2015 the Simpson Timber Company, the very heart of the Shelton economy since 1890, shut down its two mills served by the rail line.

Other than a small tourist business, VanceCreek RailRiders, which operates pedal-powered open rail cars from the Dayton mill site to a spot short of the Shelton City limits, the railroad tracks are orphaned, rusting from their abandonment.

This opens a new opportunity, however, for explorers who've always wondered what it would be like to walk the railroad tracks from downtown Shelton, all the way out to the old, former Simpson lumber mill in Dayton.

For those who want a worthy goal, rather than merely walking somewhere, let me assure you that the red railroad bridge and the Goldsborough Creek swimming hole will prove to be fine destinations, especially if you hike at a good pace on a hot, summer day.

WILD APPROACH

Now, you can park behind the Gillis Ford car dealership off Highway 101 and pick up the official Goldsborough Creek Trailhead near the power station. That will take you along the creek, upstream past the many weird, concrete fish weirs--forming a ladder of low, single-step concrete logs-- which some locals appreciate for swimming with small children.

In less than a mile you'll come to the trestle bridge that served Simpson Timber all those years. From here, make a left away from town, and follow the tracks to the bridge and swimming hole.

There is only one downside to this trail: in winter or during periods of frequent rain, the last section gets enormously wet and muddy. In summer, you're fine.

CITY APPROACH

Alternatively, you may start wherever you want from downtown Shelton, picking up the original tracks near the new Shelton greeting sign at 12th and Railroad, where the tracks, now abandoned, still cross the street.

Head away from town, following that long stretch of tracks and sidetracks, four across, that once held empty flat cars so casually they became part of the city scenery, blending in unnoticed like the smoke from the mill.

By the way, railroad ties are placed a uniform distance apart. You can match your stride and gait to them, or not. Walking between them can be just as tedious.

However, since you are committing yourself to covering several miles of tracks, let me assure you that the majority of railroad ties lie nearly level to the ground, sometimes covered with soil, but mostly nestled low between large railway gravel, step after boring step.

Since most of us never walk railroad tracks very often, this should be easy, and fun.

Heading out of town, the tracks squeeze down to a single set of rails across from Exceptional Foresters. The scenery shifts away from houses, and is soon dominated by the industrial, manmade dunes of Miles Sand & Gravel.

Time your walk right and you can pause to watch fresh stones tumble along raised conveyor belts. They make a "ching, ching, ching" sound as they go bouncing past. (I had an unnerving Fred Flintstone flashback here. Of more than coincidental value was that the only other Fred Flintstone moment in my life, ever, was getting in the pedal car at VanceCreek RailRiders, just up the tracks.)

From the tracks you get a back door industrial view. You might see trucks spraying water on the road to keep down dust from the gravel pit. As you pass beneath the Highway 101 Bridge, listen for the sounds cars make overhead, and look for long sections of exposed wooden flumes, shaped like long wine barrels wrapped in metal coils. These wooden pipes are very old and seemed to have been placed within the berm supporting the tracks, maybe from the time the railroad was first engineered. They might look like an antique collectible, but carry a strong, repulsive creosote smell.

TRESTLES ONWARD

Soon you'll come to the trestle over Goldsborough Creek, where water flows over the concrete speed bumps of the fish weir. Goldsborough Creek supports a healthy run of wild salmon.

Once on the other side, you step immediately into tall, shadowy forest. The next three miles are an exciting delight. The creek winds back and forth, disappearing for times, then running beside the tracks again.

At one point the tracks cross a retaining wall of concrete blocks on your right. Yes, this spot is deep enough for swimming, even for jumping from the lower blocks. However, the red bridge is just ahead, and shortly after that, the big culvert leading to the swimming hole on your left.

It's about three miles from downtown Shelton to the swimming hole, maybe two miles from the trestle.

Smooth, flat rocks mark the swimming hole; great places for backpacks, towels, discarded clothing. Follow the creek upstream from here and it becomes a super narrow channel of swift moving water, a magical "otterfall" of safe, playful proportions. Climb up, let go, and slide.

Goldsborough is a fairly cold creek, I'll grant you that, but this natural waterpark should inspire you to get in and get wet, no matter the initial discomfort. On a hot day, this is your lovely, refreshing reward before turning back--or if you smartly leave a car at the fire station in Dayton--continuing another three miles to your waiting vehicle.

In case you are inspired to bathe in the buff, be aware that the VanceCreek RailRiders, a popular, family oriented tourist excursion, passes by the swimming hole about eight times a day.

I'm not saying you shouldn't do it. I'm saying time it right.

The four-star swimming hole on Goldsborough Creek, which, though the trains have stopped running, is still on private, Green Diamond Resource Company property. Seek permission before attempting this hike.

58/Waterfall Witness Protection Program

If you are reading these words right now, you and I have a special connection.

You have made it to the last chapter, and are still reading, which tells me you are ready to hear a certain message.

For you, I want to share ten places of dearly beloved and well protected beauty, including three waterfalls I have chosen not to include in the body of this book. These places are special to me in ways I cannot even describe. They are either very fragile or, in the case of Lower Jorstad Falls, so easily accessible that they would soon become overrun with sudden popularity.

They are hidden, but in a perfect world they should be shared.

And while I am taking a humorous approach with my title, "The Waterfall Witness Protection Program," that is the essence of their absence in this book--to protect their location and identity.

Yet despite their fragile, special nature, people do need to experience and enjoy these places. They are wonderful and inspiring destinations, and in a most biblical way, works of beauty fashioned by God.

That's where YOU come in, dear reader.

READY TO WORK?

Despite their obvious beauty and value to humanity, each and every park in America has been "fought for" on some level. Until President Theodore Roosevelt visited John Muir at Yosemite, the fate of that magnificent land was, quite literally, up for grabs. Hundreds of other examples dot the maps of every state in America--whether indicated by a tiny green tree or other symbol--parks, monuments, forests, wilderness, recreation and wildlife preservation areas do not magically appear on their own. Plants, rocks and animals do not get a say in their own preservation. They must be fought for, appealed on behalf of, legislated for, paid for, petitioned for; because there are always those who would rather see large tracts of land converted into resource-bearing, commercial or private use.

Since Man first passed the buck in the Garden of Eden, it has always proved too tempting to convert a waterfall view or hot spring pool into a means for making money.

By contrast, it takes tremendous energy, commitment and united cooperation--usually in terms of sheer numbers--to merely *recognize* that a certain place has recreational or wilderness value, and should be preserved and made available to all.

Two success stories worth knowing about are Mono Lake, California and Winthrop in Washington. For many years, both were merely pass-through communities for travelers on their way to other, more established destinations.

However, after a majority of stakeholders were awakened by a few persistent and visionary activists, Mono Lake and Winthrop began to embrace the bicycling culture. Movement leaders tweaked and improved their message to the public, while broadening their appeal to lovers of other forms of recreation: climbers, hikers, snow skiers, even wine and gourmet aficionados.

Both areas are now four-season tourist and recreation destinations. Thet are now proud, economically healthy communities that discovered, fought for, and ultimately protected their open lands, trails and off-road exploring opportunities.

Man, that takes work!

But if you want to keep paradise and live in paradise, you need to protect it. It won't happen on its own.

GIVE TREES A CHANCE

So, where do you come in?

One of the Olympic Mountains' most beautiful creeks is little Waketickeh Creek (pronounced Wikky-Tikky) in Mason County.

Exactly 2.5 miles up the Hamma Hamma Road, you'll come to the bridge that crosses the Waketickeh. A secondary forest road juts to the right immediately after the bridge. If you park there and come back to the bridge with your river shoes and walking stick, you can begin an amazing adventure in either direction--upstream or down--slipping back in time, so to speak, as you wander through a lush riparian zone full of wild things waiting to surprise you.

You'll find no trails and almost zero signs of civilization. You will find frogs, however, and toads, snakes and the daytime sleeping blinds of deer that rose up and fled upon hearing you. You'll find a rich silence that allows you to hear the wings of a single crow flying past, or individual rocks in a symphony of riffles.

Your heart will stop when two ducks break from a calm pool, or come around the bend toward you, flying barely above the creek, honking in advance like a train blowing its horn. In both directions, you'll come upon a classic Northwest swimming hole and waterfall, too small for official naming, but far too pretty for words to describe.

At the bridge over the Waketickeh, there is a lesson to be learned. The guardrail on the south side was recently battered down by three good-sized trees, fallen in the storms of this past winter (photo below). All three trees were of harvestable size, good, healthy firs, but were left to stand as part of the riparian buffer.

The only problem was that there were no other trees left in front of them anymore, thanks to the clear cut logging, no other trees to shield them from the wind which took them down.

Now there's no riparian buffer at all. Many other trees went down in the creek, a snarl of chopsticks doing no good for wildlife, humans or harvesters. A total waste.

Many readers have hiked Big Creek Trail. Anyone who's hiked it for several years will know the spot on the left (or south) loop where the lush, mossy trail comes out suddenly into a parched, barren clear cut, like a hot, glaring slap in the face. No doubt the trail was spared, technically, by the boundary of the clear cut, but just like the Waketickeh, two and three rows of very large second-growth trees have fallen in the direction of winds they were never intended to face on their own.

The damage is compounded when falling trees take out more trees on their way down.

I visited Ilwaco recently, winding down Highway 101 through Raymond, and it's pretty clear that the "leave 'em a line along the road" is the current standard for harvest boundaries, leaving the barest fringe on a forest Brazilian.

Mile after mile, I saw the same results from the same practice: undefended, unprotected trees down everywhere, no real riparian buffers, just an audition call for sediment and erosion, two veteran actors waiting in the wings.

100 FEET OF FOREST

I'm not anti-harvest and I support timber jobs. I'd rather pound a 2-by-4 than bake an adobe brick.

But I dare to wonder aloud: Have our forest guardians and regulators slipped into a culture of laziness, "worst" practices or simply one of "looking the other way" within the National Forest Service, and to a much greater degree, the Washington Department of Natural Resources?

How can any federal or state employee stand at the Waketickeh Bridge and fill out a repair order on that guardrail without seeing the obvious: those trees would never have come down without the log harvest that left them unprotected.

The guy who walked off that timber sale ought to be given the bill for the repair.

Have they stopped teaching basic science to government employees? Without a decent buffer zone of living vegetation, steep riparian hillsides tend to collapse. Who can dispute that?

The difference is about 100 feet of forest. When walking the timber sale, give trees a chance by adding 100 feet of forest to every riparian zone.

That's not going to kill the deal. That's not condemning any loggers to the bread line. Marking off an extra 100 feet of forest will help save the most important piece of our Northwest environmental puzzle--the place where fish live, animals drink, and hundreds of species of life hold onto a watery thread.

NEED NUMBERS OF CONCERNED

I don't know exactly how we'll do it, but we need to form a new movement to save our national forests and state timber lands--in particular, the critical protection of riparian habitat.

100 Feet of Forest needs to be the message, the mantra. We need to remind our brothers and sisters on both sides of every public forest timber deal to do the right thing and give forests a fighting chance.

Currently Washington State Parks are a half-billion dollars behind in deferred maintenance, with park closures on the horizon all the time. Nearby Lake Isabella and Hoodsport Trail are no longer state parks, and more recently, Lake Cushman State Park became privately owned.

For decades the national park system has been hurting for funds.

Within Olympic National Forest--the majority focus of this book--crews, funding and equipment shortfalls are so numerous that few ranger stations are staffed fully by National Forest personnel anymore, with more and more citizen volunteers handling phones and visitor information duties.

When landslides or river flooding closes a national forest road, that road may stay closed forever. The town of Brinnon has seen a formerly main and popular driving route into Olympic National Park become a long walking trail due to a landslide that was deemed too difficult and expensive to mitigate.

For years the forest service has promised to pave the Lake Cushman road all the way to Staircase, but nothing has been done.

Last year they decommissioned lovely Oxbow Campground, taking out a single pit toilet, which will only make things decidedly worse.

With Washington State Forest (Department of Natural Resources) lands, too often it's a "blue gate" solution for managing public acreage: cut off public access with a blue steel gate, with keys only for employees and timber harvesters.

The point I am trying to make is that nearly all government agencies overseeing public lands are in deep debt or full retreat from their duties to promote and protect the land for the citizens they serve.

As stewards, they are falling woefully short.

I want to help, I want to change the status quo. And I want you to join me in reawakening our public servants to take the high road once again.

Check out my website at **wherewaterfallsare.com** so I can add you to a mailing list devoted exclusively to promoting and protecting our public parks and wilderness.

It's also an invitation to join the 100 Feet of Forest Hiking Club.

Throughout the year, you will be invited to join me on a series of very special and exclusive hikes to each of the 10 locations listed below. These are destinations too fragile or too easily overrun to be included in this book.

It is my hope that many others feel as strongly as I do about the natural environment. It is my highest dream that many more will join me in standing up for our publicly owned lands, knowing that we win the battle by fighting for 100 Feet of Forest at a time.

THE ONES THAT GOT AWAY:
10 MEMBERS OF THE WATERFALL WITNESS PROTECTION PROGRAM

Elk Lake Campsite
Hamma Hamma Campsite
Hideout Falls
Monarch Campsite
Monarch Grove/Snow Lake Trail
Lower Jorstad Falls
Decker Pond*
Lower Lilliwaup Falls*
Upper Lilliwaup Falls*
Six Tears Falls**

*Private property with single annual visit
**Single annual visit with no more than four in party

Above: Pristine, nature-protected Lower Jorstad Falls. Below: Decker Pond with reflective magic, dreamy beyond belief.

ACKNOWLEDGEMENTS

For the guys who know: Rick Endicott, Stan Graham, Ron Gold, Mike Fredson.

For the one guy who'll walk miles with me, especially if the destination is mushrooms: Chuck Pfeil.

For the original push: Pam Hanson.

For support and editorial understanding: *The Shelton-Mason County Journal.* And to all my many readers, fans, followers and friends of the forest, I appreciate your enthusiasm and letting me know there IS a connection.

For endless hours of page design and artistic skills, computer fixes and Photoshop miracles: Linda.

For a huge listening heart and the unfortunate map coordinates of being my only port for every storm, again, it's always been Linda.

Mark Woytowich is a writer, photographer and video producer who lives in Potlatch, on Hood Canal. He has devoted more than 25 years to exploring unknown parts of the Olympic National Forest, particularly the creek and river systems of the southeastern Olympic Mountains. Having grown up in the woods as a child, Mark has retained his wonder of the outdoors, communicating his love and affinity for the Olympic wilderness with wholehearted passion whenever he does a talk or presentation.

For more than four years Mark has shared his love and knowledge of the Olympic National Park and Forest as the outdoors columnist for the *Shelton-Mason County Journal*. He can be reached at wherewaterfallsare@hctc.com or through his website, www.wherewaterfallsare.com.

PHOTO COURTESY OF GEORGE STENBERG
LAYOUT & COVER DESIGN BY LINDA WOYTOWICH

Made in the USA
Columbia, SC
24 April 2019